Goal!

Goal!

How football conquered the world

Catherine Chambers

black dog

First published in 2006
This edition published in 2010 by
black dog books
15 Gertrude Street
Fitzroy Vic 3065
Australia
+61 3 9419 9406
+61 3 9419 1214 (fax)
dog@bdb.com.au
www.bdb.com.au

Cover design by Ektavo Pty Ltd
Original design by Blueboat Design
Cover photograph © Photolibrary/ Randy Faris

Internal photographs:
Page 6, Pelé, Australian Picture Library/Popperfoto; Page 43, Diego Maradona, Sport The Library; Page 78, George Best, Sport The Library; Page 95, World Cup Semi Final 1930 Uruguay, Australian Picture Library/Popperfoto; Page 96, England Soccer team Nazi salute, Australian Picture Library/Popperfoto; Page 110, Marta Vieria Da Silva, AAP Images; Page 115, Michelle Akers, Sport The Library; Page 126–127, Allianz Arena, AAP Images; Page 137, Pierluigi Collina, Sport The Library; Page 140, David Beckham, Sport The Library; Page 147, Mark Schwarzer, Sport The Library.

Printed and bound in Australia by Griffin Press
The paper in this book is sourced from Finland and manufactured under ISO 14001 certification from wood grown in certified forests. No old growth forest wood has been used in the manufacture of this book.

National Library of Australia cataloguing-in-publication data:
Chambers, Catherine, 1954-
Goal! : how football conquered the world / Catherine Chambers.
Rev. ed.
ISBN: 9781742031576 (pbk.)
Includes index.
Football--History.
796.33

10 9 8 7 6 5 4 3 2 1 10 11 12 13 14 15

FOR JOHN JOSEPH CHAMBERS
AND HIS BELOVED STOCKPORT COUNTY

CONTENTS

CHAPTER ONE

KICK START

"The roots of our Soccer Tribe lie deep in our primeval past."

Desmond Morris (1928–): zoologist, author, surrealist painter and broadcaster

PINPOINTING THE ORIGINS of football is rather like scrambling for the ball itself. "It's MINE! I got there FIRST!" Many claim it, but few can prove it. Kicking a pebble may well have been born in a prehistoric cave; we'll probably never know for sure. But with regards to a more structured game, there are written histories, archaeological finds and artworks from ancient China and Japan to Egypt, Greece, Rome, Australia and the Americas. As archaeologists work their way around the globe, they'll probably find that football's web of roots reaches almost everywhere. And while the games may vary from country to country, city to city, and school to school, the name "football" has been used for centuries, while the name "soccer" is a much more recent invention.

ANCIENT FOOTBALLING NATIONS

Central American Maya, Aztec and Olmecs

From 1500 BCE, these Meso-American peoples played games with rubber balls: some with a paddle, others with only their feet. But most popular was a game that utilised the hips, knees, elbows and backside. Olmec traders spread the game to the US's south-west by 700 CE. Some of the ball courts were dazzling white with brightly painted patterns, while 200 bare-stone oval-shaped courts have been found between the Mexican border and Arizona. The game was both a street pastime and a ritual, gladiatorial spectacle. Mayan kings even bound defeated players into a ball and bounced them down the stone steps of pyramids, to the whoops and cries of countless onlookers. These ball games lasted until the Spanish conquest in the 16th century — and longer in remote areas.

Play like an Egyptian

Some Egyptologists think that coloured cloth balls with seeds inside were booted across fields during fertility festivals. Linen balls and bouncier leather ones with catgut inside have been found inside tombs, too.

Canadian and Alaskan Inuit

The people of far-northern America played a football game on ice called *Aqsaqtuk*, that involved trying to kick a ball through a line of players and then at a goal.

Australian Aboriginal People

For thousands of years Indigenous Australians played *marn-grook*, a drop-kicking and high-catching game which was played with a possum-skin ball. High-marking, a stunning feature of modern Australian Rules football, was possibly influenced by *marn-grook*.

China

From 300 BCE, *tsu chu* involved kicking and pushing a ball with the body, but not the hands. In royal matches each team tried to kick the ball through a tiny hole in a silk net. Women played a similar game with eight players called *Eight Immortals Crossing the Sea*.

Japan

Japanese *kemari* evolved after *tsu chu* and was played by two to twelve players. The object of the game was to keep the ball in the air just using the feet — like "keepy uppy". An ancient text has recently revealed that a match took place between Chinese *tsu chu* players and a Japanese *kemari* team in 50 CE. Was this football's first international?

Ancient Europe

From 1000 BCE, football games from Greece, Rome and the Celtic cultures of England, Scotland, Wales and Ireland are probably more direct ancestors of the 19th century "modern" game developed in England and Scotland.

GREEK GOALS AND GIRLS

By the glistening blue Aegean Sea, a shriek of young women is kicking, throwing and punching — a ball, and probably each other. Hollering and heckling, diving, dodging and quite possibly slapping and tripping too, they chase the thudding ball into the waves.

"Out of play! Out of play!"

"NO! Play on!"

"But we SAID! When it smacked the sea, we SAID the ball would be out of play … "

Just another out-of-hand game of beach football? Well, no. It was in fact a popular pastime for young women about 4000 years ago in ancient Greece. Actually, men played more than women — probably because they had more time. First, the players took their clothes off in the "undressing" room, and then, totally uncluttered by clothes, these early players took to the pitch, happily naked and cheered on by the crowds.

The game we are talking about is called *Episkyros* (or *Phaininda*). It was played with a ball much the same size as a football. In the National Museum of Athens, an ancient marble relief shows an *Episkyros* player demonstrating his skills to a young lad — balancing the ball on his thigh. This scene is now reproduced on the European Cup trophy and provides a tangible link between football's past and present.

WHAT'S IN A BALL?

1. Ancient Americans from 1600 BCE learned how to process brittle rubber by adding the juice of a morning glory plant species. This made it pliable and easy to shape into a bouncy ball, which could weigh up to 7 kg.
2. Australian *marn-grook* was played with a ball made from possum skin filled with charcoal and later filled with lighter-weight possum string made of the creature's hair.
3. Early Greek balls were made from bundles of hair and cloth tied with string and sewn into the shape of a ball. Sponges — once living, oozing sea creatures — were chopped into small pieces. They, too, were wrapped in linen, tied and sewn. Their air pockets made the ball scuff and skip.
4. Much, much later, well into the 19th century, many footballs were made out of blown-up animal bladders — usually pig. They were then covered with sections of sewn leather. The result? A ball rather like the shape of an egg.

Champagne supernovas on the pitch

To mark the 100th anniversary of FIFA in 2004, the great Pelé was asked to select his top 100 players of all time. So he gave them 125. Here are some soccer legends that many footy fans might nominate, starting with Pelé himself.

He could dribble, pass, create goals and destroy goalkeepers. Scoring for classy club, Santos, at only 16, this prodigy went on to help win the World Cup for Brazil three times. He's the world's record scorer with 1281 goals in 1363 matches. Pelé was born in a place called Tres Coracoes — Three Hearts. Did they all belong to him?

Edson Arantes Do Nascimento — or just "Pelé" (meaning volcano goddess)

of Santos and Brazil (1940–)

But Brazil's mesmerising footballers can't totally rule the roost. During his playing days, even Pelé was gobsmacked by one of the best saves he'd ever seen — of his own shot! The goalkeeper? None other than the great Gordon Banks ...

The rules of *Episkyros* are hard to verify, but the ball's materials and construction are well documented. Made of an animal's bladder, usually a pig's, the ball was then wrapped in leather. It was the first recognisable soccer ball, complete with inner tube, and is depicted on the marble relief. It was called a *follis* and was an important development in the game — because it was inflated it bounced higher than earlier versions. This meant that ball-control skills changed, so that they possibly resembled those of modern soccer. Perhaps the development of fast and high-bouncing balls also demanded limits on the size of the pitch — to stop the game from spreading too far from the crowd. We don't know exactly. But by Roman times, limits certainly were defined.

Our earliest sports commentator?
According to Antiphanes, a Greek writer (408–334 BCE, or 388–311 BCE), *Episkyros* was a very skilled game with a fanatical fan base. He wrote of one player, "He seized the ball and passed it with a laugh to one, while with the other player he dodged; from one he pushed it out of the way ... amid resounding shouts of 'out of bounds, too far, over his head, on the ground, up in the air, too short, pass it back in the scrimmage'."

ROLLING ALONG WITH THE ROMANS

Episkyros was adopted and adapted by the Romans after they overwhelmed the Greek Mediterranean Empire from 146 BCE. The conquerors gave the game a facelift and a new name, *Harpastum*, which means "the game with the small ball". It is thanks to writers in Roman times that we know a little more about how this game was played and the sporting culture that surrounded it.

Normally between five and twelve players took to the pitch, which was rectangular, had sidelines and another line in the centre that split the pitch into two halves. Sounds familiar? Well, similarities to modern soccer end here. The aim of this game was to keep the ball in your own half, while the opposing team tried to wrestle it off you and take it back to their side of the central line. Only the player holding the ball could be tackled, which led to all sorts of evasive tactics and deceptions, and mostly the ball was moved using the hands. This and other Roman

Play to the death

Like all boys, those in ancient Rome played ball in the streets – and caused havoc. Once, a barber got hit by a ball, jogged the razor and killed the client he was shaving. That's according to Cicero, a Roman politician, orator and writer who lived during the time of Julius Caesar. Why do adults always blame everything on boys kicking balls in the street?

ball games — all called *pila* — resembled rugby, Celtic football, American and Canadian football, Australian Rules and *Dhada* from Rajasthan in the Indian subcontinent, far more than they did soccer. But then, as we shall see later, soccer was wrenched away from ball-handling games quite late in its history.

CELTIC KICKING

At its height in 117 BCE, the Roman Empire stretched from Portugal in the west to the Caspian Sea in the east, and from England in the north to Africa in the south. It should be no surprise then, that *Harpastum* and other *pila* found their way to the fields and lanes of their satellite states. But these lands were not without their own ball games.

In Bronze-Age England, tribes of different European origins became heavily influenced by Celtic Indo-European culture — probably through trade, and perhaps immigration. English peoples absorbed the Celtic languages, arts and customs. These included a football game, as the Romans later testified when they took to the pitch against them in a mixed match of *Harpastum* and "Celtic kicking".

BACK TO BASICS

By 446 CE the Roman Empire was dying, but not all Roman soldiers returned home. Some stayed behind, married the locals and melted into the mainstream population. Some even kept *Harpastum* alive in its original form for a while, particularly in France.

England, however, was quite a different matter. Here the Romans had done what they did best: they took a decently constructed game along decently constructed roads and spread it far and wide. But after the Romans had marched back home, English tribes did what they knew best. They returned to their own ancient, ball-belting ritual game — Celtic kicking. In those places where Romans had poor control, ancient Britons had probably never really stopped playing it. After the Romans left, the island game was probably a mixture of Celtic and *Harpastum* traditions, varying from region to region, and even town to town.

At the very least, the Romans had continued the culture of playing ball games during their occupation. They had recognised its joy and comparative innocence, and had concentrated on banning institutions more threatening to their empire, such as powerful ancient Druid priests and later, Christian ones. Football had, for the moment, continued unscathed.

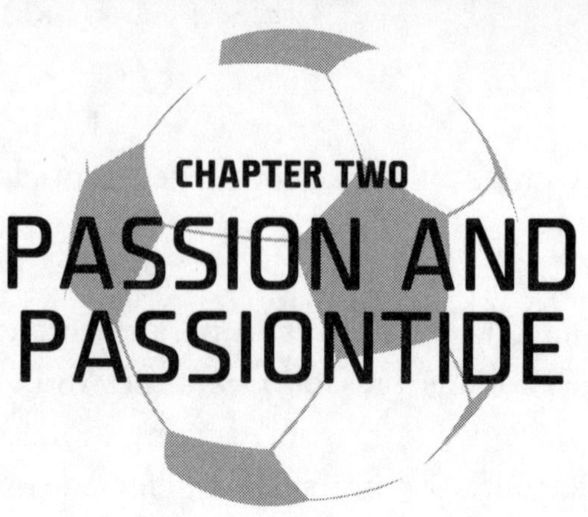

CHAPTER TWO

PASSION AND PASSIONTIDE

PRE-19TH CENTURY football was often associated with religious rites and festivals. The ball itself was at times a symbol of ritual significance and, much like modern times, football players and spectators exuded fervour and power. These features obviously weaved their way from antiquity through to the modern game. Despite the fall of the Roman Empire, English football remained a passionate pursuit through the Middle Ages, the Renaissance and well into the 18th century. Mostly it was played by ordinary folk as an everyday pastime on streets and in fields. The "big match" was saved for special occasions. These were nearly always on Christian holidays, especially the numerous saints' days and also during the run up to Easter called Passiontide.

Passiontide is the last two weeks of the forty-day fast known as Lent. Shrove Tuesday is the eve of Lent, and used to be marked by a feast of rich foods that were enjoyed before everything that's yummy had to be given up as a personal sacrifice. So people partied in a seriously big way on Shrove

Tuesday. And in old England, what better way to party than with a whopping blast of footy? One of the first pieces of English football reporting comes from this time of the year. It was written by William Fitzstephen between about 1174 and 1183 CE.

> After lunch all the youth of the city go out into the fields to take part in a ball game. The students of each school have their own ball; the workers from each city craft are also carrying their balls. Older citizens, fathers, and wealthy citizens come on horseback to watch their juniors competing, and to relive their own youth through them: you can see their inner passions aroused as they watch the action and get caught up on the fun being had by the carefree adolescents.

Things don't change. Here are so many of the ingredients found in the modern game: passion; men of all ages wanting to join in the game; and "yoofs" hanging around and having way too much fun. Importantly, we see the whole spectrum of society involved — from the artisan to the aristocrat. This too carried through to the modern game.

But what was the football of Shrovetide and saints' days like? There are actually no references to it as a kicking game until King James I of Scotland banned the game in 1424. This swipe at football gives us an indication of how dangerous and threatening it was sometimes thought to be. There is little indication of the playing skills and tactics involved though. But judging by Shrovetide games that still exist in England today, the game probably consisted of a ball being thrown, wrestled and booted from one end of a town or village to the other. Teams may have had any number of players — sometimes hundreds — grasping, throwing and kicking the ball to the finish line. This was usually someone's field, gate, garden wall — or if they were particularly unlucky — front door.

Kicking clergy

In England of old, many priests joined in football games among the gravestones after church. In 1519, a curate from Berkshire was sacked because every Sunday he babbled all his services in one swift session ... just so he could play football afterwards!

PAUPERS AND PRINCES

Football games were also played in mainland Europe. Was it Celtic or Norman culture that influenced football in the French provinces of Normandy, Picardy and Britanny? We shall probably never know, but in these provinces, *la soule* became as popular as *boule* is today. First cited in the 12th century CE, *la soule* was considered so dangerous, both physically and politically, that it was banned during the French Revolution. The game was played right up until the

Second World War and many French claim it to be the origin of modern football. Wild and ferocious, it had scrummages of countless players — and it often ended up in the water, where you could still score a goal!

Across the Alps, in the Italian city-state of Florence, the rich and titled developed fancy-dress football. Like early English football, the Italian game was played during the religious season known as the Epiphany, which started on 6 January and continued until Lent. A rather posh football game, it was called *o calcio storico*, and like the Italian masked balls of Lent, the players wore costumes. Despite this, the game involved a lot of kicking and wrestling, and there were written rules. Somehow it became highly fashionable among the aristocracy and upper-middle classes of other nations such as England, and there it boosted football's popularity among the well-to-do.

BAN THE BALL!

In Mediaeval and Renaissance times, plagues took at least a third of Europe's population — two-thirds in some parts. Wars wasted many soldiers' lives and disrupted farming, causing widespread famine, disease and the death of many people. Rulers had to re-establish stability, law and order, and football was seen as counterproductive. New soldiers had to be recruited and football, which was once encouraged

The only way was up after a young Banks let in 15 goals in two games for England's Yorkshire League club, Romarsh Welfare. But he's a perfect example of why we should never quit. For he is thought by many to be the best goalkeeper of all time — playing as an international for ten consecutive years.

Gordon Banks

of Stoke and England (1937–)

The save against Pelé was a finger-tip touch to a confident, seemingly perfect header. Banks was a World Cup winner in 1966. But he couldn't have done his job without one of the best defenders and tacticians of all time — the great Bobby Moore ...

SEE PAGE 23 FOR BOBBY MOORE

as a training game for soldiers, was now considered a distraction from "real" fighting skills like archery.

While football was a rare bit of fun in peoples' short and often painful lives, it was invariably condemned as a source of anarchy. Booting a ball could easily turn into a mob kicking in the door of their local baron (and then the gate of their king or queen). So in the light of all this negativity, football became banned in many parts of England and mainland Europe. In England, it was outlawed off and on for over 500 years — from the 12th to the 17th century. And in some areas, even beyond that. But this wasn't the same for Ireland. Here, the 1527 Statute of Galway — referring to the County of Galway — allowed for "the great foote balle" and archery, but forbade other sports such as the ball-and-stick game of hurling.

Women winners

During the last half of the 17th century, married women played football against unmarried women in Inveresk, Scotland. The married women usually won. Was this because they were the better team? Or were they fighting to prove that marriage was "the right thing to do"?

IT'S NOT "PROPER"

It was around this time that the English King Henry VIII changed the faith of the nation from Catholicism to Anglicanism — largely for his own convenience. This change meant that countless Catholic saints' days got clobbered — as did the football frolics that often went with them. Christianity became plainer, quieter, more pious and puritanical. Dare we say, a little dull? Football was soon considered to be a yobbish, dangerous pastime played by people with nothing better to do. The Sunday game was declared a SIN.

What's more, Henry got extremely irritated by a game that usually ended up with smashed windows. So he re-enacted previous laws that banned the ball. Yet from his reign until the mid-18th century it continued to be played with defiance and enthusiasm — despite the fact that punishments for playing it could be quite harsh. He is also rumoured to have played himself.

Guilty goals
Queen Elizabeth I of England passed a law insisting that football players be "jailed for a week and obliged to do penance in church". Hmmm. Church? Did the guilty play yet another game after paying their penance?

In Manchester in 1618, special football officers were appointed to deal with "lewd and disordered" street football players. Organisers of football games and even spectators were prosecuted for their involvement. Pursed-lipped Puritans deplored it. Members of Parliament decried it. Added to this was a huge swing in economic misfortune for the masses. The "game for all" (and for all occasions) would have to change by the end of the 18th century. Like the brutalised working classes who played it, football faced huge odds against its survival. But the big game just would not lie down and die. Indeed, through England's colonial ambitions it would begin to take root across the globe.

From the 17th century onwards, Shrovetide-style football took root in many of England's, and later Great Britain's (since 1707), overseas colonies and outposts. Settlers, sailors and traders brought their versions of the game to their adopted homes, and many encountered similar games already rooted in the local cultures.

Football was reported in England's American settlement of Jamestown as early as 1609. But it was frowned upon as a bad influence and promptly banned. A local American ball game called *Pahsaheman* was also recorded at about this time. That was probably banned, too. But football gathered silent strength — often in the most unlikely places. In early 18th century America, football was taken-up by the educated sons of the rich and powerful. In Britain too, public schoolboys and university students seized football by the scruff of its neck and turned it into a game with a system; while the working classes began to find it difficult to play at all.

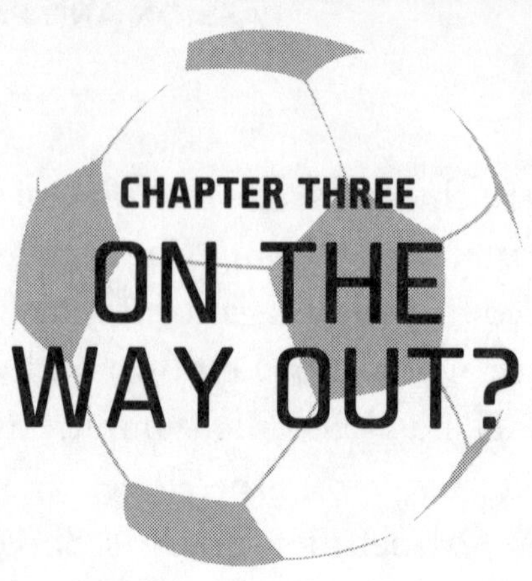

CHAPTER THREE

ON THE WAY OUT?

BY THE BEGINNING of the 19th century, the working classes had even less time and energy to play football — or indeed, anything at all. From the last half of the 18th century, the Industrial Revolution had sucked the poor and the hopeful into factories and mills, onto rail tracks and along roadways. Well into the 19th century, powerful industrialists made England's workers toil for up to sixteen hours a day, six days a week, and in conditions not fit for a rat. (There were plenty of those too.) But if the ruling classes thought that football for the masses was finished, they were wrong. Because there was always the seventh day: the day of God — and goals. On their only day off, workers took to any open space and played the time-honoured, much scorned, Sunday football game. A game of much throwing, kicking, catching and hacking (which was the rather unkind habit of kicking someone below the knee).

Throughout the 19th century, various Factory Acts gradually reduced the working hours of women and children. By 1844 they had got down to (only!) ten hours of work a day, and factory schools opened to give children a few hours of education each week. It wasn't much and it wasn't that effective, but these and other policies showed a growing recognition that time off and recreation were good for productivity. A handful of politicians and pushy priests actually cared about the workers, too. To these ends, a half-day Saturday was introduced. Saturday afternoons were free. So what did many men and boys do? They went out and played football, of course.

The 1861 census of England and Wales shows that most people now lived in industrial cities — the majority of which were in the north. In spite of the hardships endured by these city-dwellers, men and boys always fitted in a game of footy — either playing or watching. What's more, northerners not only handled the ball, they began to dribble it — by kicking it in front of them as they ran. All this was helped by the advent of parks that had short grass.

In the 1840s, in Manchester and Salford, public parks gave public sport a venue. So did those in Sheffield. Businesses such as Cadburys, the chocolate makers, even applied their compassionate Christian Quaker principles and developed green spaces for their workforce to enjoy. Leisure, including football, was slowly making it on to the agenda.

FOOTBALL ON THE FARM

While football's popularity was growing in the cities, would football still be played by those left in the countryside? Yes, but in a rather withered way. The hundreds who churned up the mud on regular holy days were reduced to a few dozen souls on a short Sunday afternoon. Country folk were busy growing mountains of cereal and grazing larger herds of livestock to feed the rapidly expanding populations in the industrialised cities. Most farmers and labourers were absorbed into this massive rural economy, while others fled to the city to find a job.

For the country folk who stayed behind, there wasn't much free time after harvesting, storing, drying, salting and making preserves. In a society where the poor were increasingly asked for payment in cash not kind, most farm workers needed to take on extra work that paid a wage, not a sack of potatoes. The old order had changed forever, and with it, the pattern of playing football. Keeping a job to pay for the increased rents and taxes and higher prices for food were the chief concerns of the English working classes.

CAMP-BALL CAPERS

If the amount of hard work diverting people's attention from football wasn't enough, there was more bad news for that game played by the ploughman and the apple picker, the village

Winner not only of the World Cup but also the European Cup Winners' Cup (1965), Moore captained England a record 90 times. But more than this, the West Ham left-half stunned forwards with his elegant and perfectly timed tackles; his calm poise as he cleared the ball.

Bobby Moore

of West Ham and England (1941–1993)

It was Moore who made England manager Alf Ramsey's "new" 4–4–2 formation work for the national team because he could read the game like a chess master. But Moore would have needed all his intelligence to outwit Johann Cruyff ...

cartwright's apprentice and the hammerman's son. What would happen to the rural football frenzy of feast and festival? The hearty "camp-ball" game played on huge tracts of "camping" land? Well, as a Shrovetide game it was still played well into the 19th century, but not without a lot of opposition.

In the early 19th century the game faced a devastating setback when a match at Diss in Norfolk went horribly wrong. Nine men were killed in the battle for the ball. Was this a game or a territorial bloodbath? Death and football had their first big public airing. People had died before, and would do so, sadly, in the future. But the toll was so huge that public support for camp-ball declined.

Mad mayors

In 1746, Derby's Mayor Humphrey Booth banned Shrovetide football, saying it might spread foot-and-mouth disease among the local cattle. Nearly 100 years later in 1846, another mayor who came bounding in on horseback to break up the game was stoned by a screaming mob, and got so angry that he called in the troops. The next year, no-one bothered turning up to play.

A less violent "light football" took the place of the pacey, punchy games of the past. It was also confined to a smaller area, to fields of moderate size, and teams had less players. Even though the number "eleven" is bandied about a lot by historians, anywhere from ten to thirty players still joined a team at any one time. But if some teams really did play with eleven men and boys, were these the same eleven that played as a cricket team during the summer months? It could be that the players of light football helped mould the football game that we know today.

THE SEEDS OF SOCCER

The slightly less rugged game played after church on Sunday fitted in with the new economy, with law and order, and within a small field far better than Shrovetide football ever had.

We don't know if this game had any special rules, but we know that there was more kicking and less running with the ball. Players had less space to work with, so running for miles was no longer an option. This tighter, more restricted game became better organised too. Villages and towns set up fixtures with one another. Maybe, like early cricket games, local "gentlemen" played "the rest" — the town or village artisans and labourers. This type of game soon became so important that teams touted for the best footballers they could find. In doing so, some invited ex-public schoolboys and university students to play for them. Why? Because they were good and passionate sports. And also because the university players were getting their act together in terms of organisation, and setting down rules and standards.

CHAPTER FOUR

A SPORT FOR KINGS?

"Football is all very well as a game for rough girls, but is hardly suitable for delicate boys."

Oscar Wilde (1856–1900): Irish poet and playwright

IN 19TH CENTURY Britain, many in the working classes thought posh public schoolboys were a little too delicate. But the reality was that the sons of the rich and titled were just as fired up as anyone. Ball games, a form of rather violent boxing, and other similar sports had always been played by the elite, independent "grammar", or "public" schools of England and Scotland.

Winchester School, founded in the 10th century, was the first to document an early ball game, played with hands as well as feet. At first, these games weren't organised — they were just something to do outside the rather riotous classroom. But soon teachers co-opted these games for their own ends.

TAMING THE TEENAGERS

In the 1830s, English public schoolmasters, led by the headmasters of Rugby and Shrewsbury, believed that their boys' limp moping and occasional savagery was a sickness that needed to be cured.

The medicine? A game that required a tough physical regime to keep the boys fit and healthy. One that needed a lot of practice, giving the "athletes" less time to flop around, drink, gamble and poach pheasants from the grand houses around them. It would be a competitive game to release all that latent aggression — and occasionally it would be released on boys from other, rival public schools. Lastly, it would be a game that included a few knocks to "develop character" and self-discipline. In those days, boys simply *could not* cry.

In fact, in the eyes of the parents, football was a form of career preparation for their offspring. Many sons later became officers in the armed forces, so the football pitch was a taste of the battlefield to come. For most people, football fitted the bill perfectly.

ROUGH AND READY

In 1831, an anonymous Etonian wrote in his memoir, *Eton. By an Old Etonian*:

> I cannot consider the game of football as being at all gentlemanly. It is a game which common people of Yorkshire are particularly partial to, the tips of their shoes being heavily shod with iron: and frequently death has been known to ensue from

A giant for club Ajax, Cruyff scored 33 times for Holland. Was he a centre forward? Or a midfielder? Or a winger? Well, it didn't really matter.

Johann Cruyff

of Ajax and Holland (1947–)

This total player with multiple skills, finesse and frightening fitness could work himself into a different position and still make magic. He needed to against this next opponent — Gerd Muller.

SEE PAGE 33 FOR GERD MULLER

the severity of the blows inflicted thereby.

This young Etonian must have spent all his time bent over books. If he'd just looked up for a moment he might have seen his fellow students having fun and booting a ball around outside. His scathing snobbery towards the people of Yorkshire shows how little he knew about the game played by other public schools. For up in the English Midlands, Rugby School footballers also chose to wear iron-tipped boots. In any case, perhaps we shouldn't take too much notice of someone who can't think up a more imaginative title to his memoir, although he was right about one thing.

Football was horrendously rough. Eton players recognised this as early as 1815, when they introduced a few rules. And soon other schools forged their own. The problem was, though, that each school had a different set. So later, when they played each other, they spent quite some time agreeing on their code of play for that particular match. Perhaps this was the first need for a referee?

MATCH MAKING

What did an average schoolboy football game look like? Well, most began with a "bully" — a type of scrimmage or scrum. After scrambling for the ball within the scrum, one player ended up with it. The ball was then tossed, usually behind, or dribbled, usually ahead, towards the "goal". This was often a line, imaginary or otherwise, at the end of a field. Perhaps the goal was between two trees, hedges or buildings; sometimes the goal was two sticks stuck in the ground. At this stage each school team had its own ideas on the finer points of the game — on offside rules, tackling guidelines, ball-handling, ball out-of-play and so on. But from about the 1830s through to the 1860s, public school codes were developing and diverging into two distinct camps.

One camp had more dribbling than handling, and the other more handling than dribbling. One had less hacking — the other, as much hacking as possible. Some of these differences developed from environmental factors — such as the size and position of the pitch. Others grew from tradition, whim and the imagination.

TO DRIBBLE ...?

How do you play football in a confined space? Perhaps in the back yard, or a narrow street? You can't run far with the ball, nor boot it into oblivion. You have to dribble it, trying to outwit your opponent with dodging and quick passing. Footballers in schools with small outdoor spaces were often forced to develop the game along these lines. There were still scrums and ball-handling, but far less than in games played in open fields.

Football at Charterhouse School developed within a cramped, city environment. From 1611 to 1873, the school's London site restricted games to courtyard areas. Matches between students were held in the "cloisters" — a long, bare, narrow corridor. About fifty boys charged along the stone floor, dodging the buttresses and jagged flint walls. At each end, a quiver of young, small and very frightened "slaves" defended the goals, which were wooden doors. Although the players often ended up in a brawling heap of a scrum, the ball was actually dribbled up and down the flagstones for some of the time.

Charterhouse champions
Charterhouse School championed the game of football with its "Charterhouse Rules" in the 1840s. Later, with Winchester School pupils and ex-pupils, it loudly defended the "dribbling code", which led to football as we know it today.

Eton, on the other hand, had spacious playing fields as well as walled grounds. When the school was organised into "houses" in the 19th century (representing different groups of students), each house had its own field. Football became competitive between boys from each house, and importantly, it became more open. The game began with a scrum. Then the ball was worked by the feet across the field to the goal line. A kicked goal scored three points: a touch-down goal, only one. The team that scored the touch-down goal could then gain two more points if they managed to work the ball over the line whilst in a scrum with the opposite side — rather like modern rugby's "drive tries".

Football – that great learning tool

In 1633, Aberdeen Grammar School employed a very imaginative master, David Wedderburn. He used football to encourage his pupils to learn difficult Latin phrases. They included phrases that were translated as: "kick off so that we can begin the match"; "you keep goal"; "get hold of the ball if you can manage it"; "charge him!"; and "pass the ball back". While Latin as a language may be fading away, these phrases give us a great indication of how 17th century soccer was played.

You can see from the goal-scoring that kicking and foot skills were highly valued. The two-point goal seems almost like converting a try in rugby football. In fact, quite a lot of the game reminds me of rugby. But in none of the games described so far could you run with the ball, which is very relevant to the way football developed later.

OR NOT TO DRIBBLE ...?

Rugby, Shrewsbury and other schools set in large grounds played the kind of football found on village greens throughout the land. There was a scrum, or a "squash", as it was known at Shrewsbury. Then players caught and kicked the ball towards the goal line. But running with the ball was

"The Bomber wrote records for eternity." That just about sums up this lightning centre-forward who pounced on the ball and fired shots like bullets in the penalty area. Muller led the rise of mighty Bayern Munich with 365 goals in 427 Bundesliga appearances. And 68 goals in 62 games for his country.

Gerd Muller

of Bayern Munich and West Germany (1945–)

He was top-scorer in the 1970 World Cup with ten goals and top club scorer from 1964 to 1978. But this legend had to put up with all sorts of unnecessary remarks about his seemingly short legs and stocky build. So, too, did this next marksman, Diego Armando Maradona.

SEE PAGE 43 FOR DIEGO MARADONA

still banned until the 1841–42 season, when Rubgy School decide to include it officially in their rules. Rugby School had laid the foundations of that great game of the same name played today.

AFTER-SCHOOL FOOTBALL

Like spinning tops, many ex-public schoolboys whirled around the world, footballs in hand — as captains and generals, diplomats and viceroys, merchants and engineers, colonisers and plantation owners. Others became civil servants, or bankers and businessmen in London, and other major British cities and ports: Bristol, Liverpool, Manchester, Glasgow. Here they came into contact with people from all over the world, whose own football traditions lay waiting for a new boost.

The seed that would lead to the "World Game" was beginning to take root. But it was struggling in stony soil. There was no firm set of rules. The game needed to be organised, and by people who had nothing better to do with their time. So, enter all those public schoolboys who became university students. As we shall see, modern football owes them big time. But student footballers didn't always have a smooth ride …

BAN THE BALL — AGAIN!

University students had played football for centuries. At times, they played matches against local townsmen and villagers. As early as 1579, Cambridge University students are recorded playing an "away" match in the village of Chesterton. The villagers, though, decided to welcome their visitors by attacking them with pikes. One of the "home" team's players was a police constable called Thomas Parishe, who ordered the locals to stop. After all, gouging with spikes was going just a bit too far.

But many Cambridge students were highly skilled footballers, and town and village teams even "borrowed" them on occasion. Nevertheless, after this footy fracas, all university away matches were banned in 1580 and 1581. Breaking these university rules in 1584 led to fines and getting chucked out of university. But football carried on, even though university football continued to be rough, destructive and rarely safe.

Famous football players

Oliver Cromwell (1599–1658) attended Cambridge University from 1616 to 1617. There he was described as "one of the chief match makers and players at football, cudgels or any other boystrong sport or game". Later he banned football. There is a story that his own severed head was kicked around the streets of London.

King Charles I of England, Scotland and Ireland (1600–40) was a great sports fan. As such, he smiled on football, reissuing the Declaration of Sports that allowed it to be played. But that said, in 1636 he banned football for university students. Perhaps he expected "better things" from them. Perhaps, as the nation's future ruling class, they should show more responsibility — and dignity?

FRACTURED FOOTBALL

By the beginning of the 19th century, laws against university football were relaxed. Players from public schools took their kit and their rules up to their university colleges. But this posed a problem. Students were trained in many different public school football traditions. This made it hard for them to finish a game without arguing over what was fair and what was not. The crunch had come.

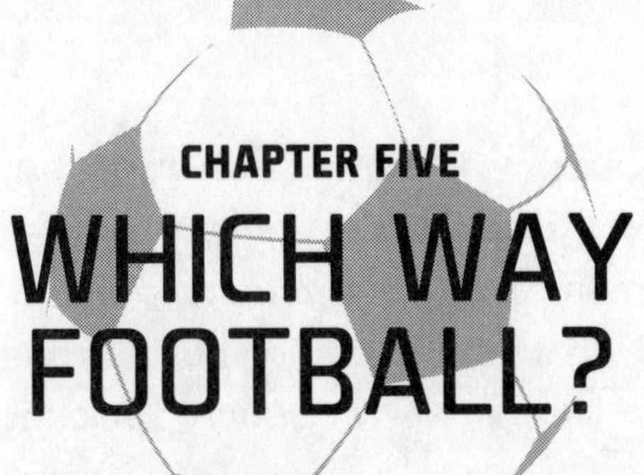

CHAPTER FIVE

WHICH WAY FOOTBALL?

"The rules of soccer are very simple, basically it is this: if it moves, kick it. If it doesn't move, kick it until it does."

Phil Woosnam (1932–): Welsh footballer and US soccer coach and advisor

TO CARRY THE BALL and throw it, or dribble and kick it? Or both? To hack shins, trip feet and pull shirts? Or to let the fellow go? These were the battles faced in the mid-19th century by football teams throughout England, whether in village or town, school or university. Scrumming, hacking, and handling were Rugby rules. They had been adopted and adapted by many clubs. But some players preferred to concentrate on foot skills. There were major differences between teams and team members. It all needed sorting out.

CAMBRIDGE RULES AND RAGES

In 1846 and 1848, student players met at Trinity College, Cambridge to thrash out some basic rules. The main issues were handling and hacking. In 1848 the ex-Rugby School boys were all for them, but the

Charterhouse, Winchester and Eton boys, among others, were dead against them.

Two main principles emerged from the fray. One was that there could be tackling, but no heavy hacking. That is, no violent tripping, punching, charging, strangling or any other movement that toppled the opponent violently to the ground. The other was that the ball could be caught by hand, if the ball had been kicked into the air. But then it had to be dropped straight to the ground and moved with the feet or nudged by another part of the body. In other words, you couldn't catch the ball and run off with it.

Offside

Most mid-19th century games had an "off his side" rule that stopped attackers from lurking near the goal, waiting to pop the ball in. So basically, there was no forward passing. The 1848 Cambridge Rules even insisted on three defenders standing between the attacker with the ball and the goal.

From this time on, Cambridge University footballers took their new rules with them wherever they went. Just in time too — for football was becoming a fashionable spectator and participation sport among all the classes, and the trickle of football clubs would soon become a river. But for the moment each club still tended to follow either rugby-style football, or something more like the kicking game shaped by the Cambridge Rules. And although each borrowed bits from the other, two different codes were developing.

A CLEARER CODE

One of the most important things about the 1848 Cambridge Rules was the people who had attended the meeting that spawned them; and this included Edward Thring. In 1862, Thring's ongoing passion for football inspired him to set down the first set of detailed rules for what he called "the Simplest Game".

THE SIMPLEST GAME – THRING'S RULES

1. A goal is scored whenever the ball is forced through the goal and under the bar, except it be thrown by hand.
2. Hands may be used only to stop a ball and place it on the ground before the feet.
3. Kicks may be aimed only at the ball.
4. A player may not kick the ball whilst in the air.
5. No tripping up or heel kicking allowed.
6. Whenever a ball is kicked beyond the side flags, it must be returned by the player who kicked it, from the spot it passed the flag line, in a straight line towards the middle of the ground.
7. When a ball is kicked behind the line of goal, it shall be kicked off from that line by one of the side whose goal it is.

8. No player may stand within six paces of the kicker when he is kicking off.

9. A player is "out of play" immediately he is in front of the ball and must return behind the ball as soon as possible. If the ball is kicked by his own side past a player, he may not touch or kick it, or advance, until one of the other side has first kicked it, or one of his own side has been able to kick it on a level with, or in front of him.

10. No charging allowed when a player is "out of play"; that is, immediately the ball is behind him.

But what were the penalties for infringements of these rules? How was a match to be refereed? How many players could be on the pitch at one time? How long were the matches — and the pitches? What kind of ball could be used? These and many other aspects of the modern game had yet to be decided.

NO HACKING, TRIPPING OR HOLDING

With so many issues still to thrash out, eleven clubs and schools met around a table in the Freemason's Tavern in London on 26 October 1863. Most were London clubs, or near enough, and at the first meeting, Ebenezer Cobb Morley proposed a motion to form the London Football Association (LFA). It was a momentous occasion for football. The motion was carried eleven votes to one. The LFA was born, and the rules were thrashed out under this new organisation's banner.

Ball ballads

A Brighton College song sang of the many football shapes and sizes used: "And Eton may play with a pill if they please / And Harrow may stick to their Cheshire Cheese / And Rugby their outgrown egg. / But here, is the perfect game of the perfect sphere."

SPLITS AND STROPS

This was the first of six intense meetings that lasted from October to December of that same year. Some of them were matches in their own right. After a month of negotiations one of the clubs, Blackheath Football Club, was unhappy with some of the decisions taken — particularly on hacking — and it left the meetings at the tavern, and the newly formed LFA forever. Renaming itself the Blackheath Rugby Club, in 1871 Blackheath helped

Fast as an arrow and with a deadly left foot, Maradona could surprise with the right as well. A scorer, a feeder and a goal creator, Maradona delighted fans and devastated foes. His second goal against England in the 1986 quarter final was voted the best ever World Cup goal in a 2002 FIFA poll.

Diego Armando Maradona

of Barcelona, Napoli and Argentina (1960–)

He scored it after dribbling and dodging half the length of the pitch, passing five defenders and then shooting the ball past a normally great goalkeeper, Peter Shilton. But was Maradona the magician a "complete" footballer like the amazing Zizou …?

SEE PAGE 50 FOR ZINADINE ZIDANE

form the Rugby Football Union — a move copied later in other parts of the football-playing world.

Without the constant clamourings of the rugbyites, football mostly with feet and without "fouling" won the day. Seventeen rules covered many aspects of the game. Players were to number no more than 25. They were to play on a pitch 110 metres by 70 and shoot at a goal 22 metres wide. Handling the ball was still allowed, and it only petered out of the game in 1869. The rules were still in their infancy, but the modern game of football was definitely taking shape. And it had cracked away from rugby.

Who said "soccer"?
Charles Wreford Brown from Oxford University first used the word "soccer" in the 1880s for a bit of a laugh. It was derived from the middle bit of "Association". The name successfully distinguished football from rugby – and Wreford Brown went on to play "soccer" for England.

The first official LFA game was played in Battersea Park on 9 January 1864. The LFA President's team beat the Football Association Secretary's team 2–0. Three years later on the same ground, the LFA organised the first county match between Middlesex and a mixed team of Surrey and Kent. A journalist describing the effect of the "pitch" on the match said, "the grass, which was several inches long and extremely thick, effectively prevented all attempts at dribbling, or any exhibition of the quick play which we might have expected". "Expected" is the crucial word here. The passionate supporters of the game had high hopes for their heroes' skills. They wanted to watch fine footwork and running with the ball — along the ground. Football was defining and refining itself very quickly indeed.

NEVER FORGET THE NORTH

While the newly established London Football Association supported the growth of football in the south of England, meanwhile, in the northern cities, football was forging ahead at a furious pace. A Sheffield team got together in the 1850s as a knockabout side, but by 1857 had declared itself a proper club. Notts County emerged a little later, in 1865. Sheffield's and Notts County's original members were largely professional men who were mostly ex-public schoolboys. The crowd watching them, though, included factory and railway workers, labourers and street hawkers. They too had been knocking a ball about in new green city spaces, and were enthusiastic players as well as spectators. They too wanted to form competitive teams.

So as the 1860s wore on, football teams and supporters in Sheffield grew in passion and numbers. In 1867 the Sheffield and Hallamshire County Football Association was formed, drawing the county's various clubs together. It would have been great if they could have linked up with the south's Football Association in a friendly, group hug. But the Sheffield Association members played a purer kicking game and had different ideas about offside. They were not going to agree to play by the southerners' FA's rules. Not yet, anyway.

OVER THE OCEAN

How did all this affect the rest of the footballing world? In the United States, the fog of football rules was also coming clear in the 19th century. Players there had their own movers and shakers, and didn't need any help from Great Britain. In some ways their development of the game mirrored that from across the Atlantic. "Folk football" was rather like the old Shrovetide bash and was banned, except in remote places where there was little law enforcement. Early 19th century matches were played, as in England and Scotland, by the sons of the wealthy and in some of the most famous colleges in America's north-east.

From the 1820s, Harvard University's first- and second-year students played each other on the first Monday of the new academic year. Known as "Bloody Monday", it would be an understatement to say that the matches were hard fought. We know that both ball-handling and hacking were felt necessary to the game. At Princeton University, they had their game "ballown", which was a fist-punching and kicking version — of the ball and of each other. There were almost as many varieties of football as there were different institutions — most played within each university and often on special occasions, rather than as frequent fixtures.

GOING ALONE

In 1866 the rules for both football and rugby were printed by Beadle and Company of New York, and at first, universities were happy to experiment with both. But taking ball-handling out of the game left many non-British football players cold. They turned their back on the LFA and worked out what was most important to them. American Football, Australian Rules and others developed like rugby, as ball-handling games. Tackling remained robust and footballs flew high — and many of them ended up oval rather than round.

Football, as we'd come to know it, simmered in the background in countries around the world. Deserted by many of the educated classes, it was seized upon by the workers, who ran off with it and made it their own. By the end of the 19th century, the game was seeping, then sweeping into cities, towns and remote villages across the globe. And in Britain itself, the game was getting itself organised with breathtaking speed.

CHAPTER SIX

GETTING TOGETHER – AND GOING PRO

"Five days shalt thou labour, as the Bible says. The seventh day is the Lord thy God's. The sixth day is for football."

Anthony Burgess (1917–93): novelist, composer and journalist

WHO'D WIN THE FIGHT for football at the end of the 19th century? Would football be a game for the impoverished, toiling masses, or the privileged few? Could it be for both? Like the working-men's clubs and the trades unions, football clubs became part of working-class mass culture. Ex-public schoolboys bowed out of the modern game, which changed rapidly from being a passionate pastime into a professional career. But how did all this happen?

THE CONQUERORS' CUP

By 1871, the two handfuls of clubs belonging to the London Football Association had mushroomed to fifty. In this same year, Charles Alcock of the LFA set up one of the greatest competitions of all time for its clubs: the English Football Association's Cup. In the first season just fifteen of these clubs competed.

By 1905 there were about 10 000 FA members and 272 teams entered the competition.

The Cup started off in 1871 largely as a London affair, with a couple of exceptions. At first, public schools' "old boys' clubs" dominated it. The Old Etonians won the Football Cup twice. Then there were the rather zany Wanderers — an eccentric, rootless bunch of ex-pupils from different public schools, who lifted the Cup once in its history.

But outside this rather narrow region of England and even narrower social background, strange things were happening: artisans, labourers, factory hands and millworkers across the islands were forming small town and city teams. These little teams soon realised the power of joining together to make big, strong clubs. They were gagging to compete in the Cup. So, in the end, were the Sheffield Football Association's members from the north, who joined the London FA in 1877. By 1879 there were so many clubs competing in the Cup that the LFA had to set up elimination rounds. Expanding railway networks made it much easier for teams to accept distant away fixtures, although it wasn't always quite so easy to find the ticket money.

A RAPID RISE

The standard of play was soaring up and down the isles. The playing field between the "haves" and the "have-nots" was levelling out. Darwen,

Called a "flashy" midfielder, "Zizou" as he's known, is just breathtaking to watch. He can dribble for miles, swerve and dodge, tackle and score. Many see him as the most complete player ever. And he knows when to press the accelerator.

Zinadine Zidane

Juventus, Real Madrid and France (1972–)

In France's 1998 World Cup victory, Zidane scored twice. World Player of the year in 1998, 2000 and 2003, he competes for many honours with another Brazilian, Ronaldo Luiz Nazario de Lima.

SEE PAGE 59 FOR RONALDO

a tiny town in Lancashire, took its millworkers' team to play the Old Etonians in the 1878 Cup. It held them to a draw twice. But the millworkers had run out of money. How could they afford to tackle the Etonians for a third time? No need to worry — football was gripping the nation. Money for these underdogs poured in from the public and Darwen made it to the match. They then lost to the experienced ex-public school team, but the writing was on the wall: all teams, however small, were a dangerous threat to the old guard. In 1883 the Old Etonians lost 2–0 to Blackburn Olympic. This was the beginning of the end of the soccer supremacy of the ex-public school players. Much was owed to the public schools: countless ex-pupils had set up and supported the clubs that we know today; they upheld them financially, with great emotion and undying devotion. Many still do.

HOW WERE THE FIRST CLUBS BORN?

NOTTINGHAM FOREST (1865)	Believed to have begun as a "shinney" (hockey) team.
QUEEN'S PARK, GLASGOW (1867)	A Scottish amateur club, both then and now. Based at the famous Hampden Park, Scotland's National Stadium, it played in the early English FA Cup.
SHEFFIELD WEDNESDAY (1870)	Started as a cricket club made up of workers with only Wednesday afternoons off. Some athletics clubs branched out into football as well. Otherwise, what were cricketers and athletes supposed to do in the winter?
ASTON VILLA (1874)	Started under a street gas lamp by four members of the local Wesleyan Methodist Church cricket team.
BIRMINGHAM (1875)	Originally the Small Heath Alliance — and it really was small. They played on wasteland.
MANCHESTER UNITED (1878)	Began life as Newton Heath, a club of Lancashire and Yorkshire railway workers. In 1898, it set up the first professional footballers' trade union.

COVENTRY CITY (1883)	A club for workers at the famous Singer cycle manufacturers.
GLASGOW RANGERS (1885)	Four Glaswegians with no money and no ball decided to set up one of Scotland's most famous clubs.
QUEEN'S PARK RANGERS (1885)	It was the very good idea of the Reverend Gordon Young, who wanted to keep kids off the streets. Teachers had similar ideas.
ARSENAL (1888)	First called "Dial Square". It was set up by a Scot for northern weapons workers at Woolwich, by London's River Thames. The penniless team had to borrow red jerseys from Nottingham Forest. Arsenal's grandstand? Two military wagons.
CELTIC (1888)	Another Scottish Glasgow team, this time started by Irish Catholic immigrants to help their own desperate poor.
STOCKPORT COUNTY (1890)	Heaton Norris Rovers and Heaton Norris planned a merger to create Stockport County (known as the Hatters) in one of its many corner cafes.

GOING PRO

The victorious Blackburn Olympic team had won against all odds. Its members were mostly from the poorer working classes — the team included four millworkers, a picture framer, a metal worker, a master plumber, a dentist's assistant and two mysterious others. No-one knew exactly what these last two did apart from the fact that they played football rather well. Everyone knew that they would have had their basic expenses paid, as this was allowed after 1881 under new FA regulations. But how did these footballers make a proper living? How did they feed their families? Well, it was rumoured that they were actually paid to play football. But this was professionalism, and only amateur footballers could represent LFA teams.

Amateurism was all well and good for well-heeled ex-public schoolboys and university students. But the problem for poor and unemployed workers was made very clear by this advertisement placed in the *Leeds Mercury* as early as 7 March 1864:

> FOOTBALL — Wanted. A number of persons to form a football club for playing on Woodhouse Moor for a few days a week from 7 to 8 o'clock a.m. Apply K99 Mercury Office.

Seven a.m.! How on earth were working men supposed to train from the crack of dawn, do a full, gruelling week's grind in a factory or mill, and then take to the pitch on a Saturday afternoon? Well, with difficulty. These players needed to be paid to do just one job well. And that job was going to be football.

From the clubs' point of view, the very best players had to be attracted to the game — somehow. The ballooning crowds needed to be satisfied. Cups and medals had to be won and money made to pay for renting grounds and facilities. Amateurs couldn't devote the time needed to achieve all this. So clubs with working-class players began to pay them, and began to organise their teams on a more professional basis. This created a huge gulf between them and the traditional clubs, who refused to play with paid players, or against them.

Dazzling amateurs

Oh, the Corinthians! What an exceptional, posh amateur side – modelled on the eccentric Wanderers. The Corinthians were not interested in the FA Cup, but they challenged any team that would play them. The club took British soccer to South Africa in 1897, playing twenty-three teams. Charles Wreford Brown was one of its stars and the Corinthians are still playing today.

To many professional clubs, the LFA's ex-public school footballers and organisers suddenly looked quirky, shambolic and frankly, amateurish. Football cultures cracked apart. A chasm opened between the paid and the unpaid — and between the different social classes. When the LFA caved in to professionalism in 1885, it was much too late for many amateurs to remain in the top-class game. The gulf between them and the professionals was now far too wide.

EYES TO THE NORTH

Clubs didn't want to pay just any old players — they had particular stars in mind. And most of these came from Scotland. Why? Because Scottish football players had begun to do something really special with the ball. They passed it as well as dribbled it. In fact, they had to, because winter in the north meant claggy, sticky soils — and you just can't dribble well on them. Passing led to a much faster and more exciting game. A real crowd-pleaser, and thus a money-magnet. Luckily for England, the Scottish FA resisted professionalism for even longer than the English FA. So Scottish players trudged southward, hoping for more than just a few coins stuffed down the side of their boots in "boot-money expenses".

Famous footballers

In the 1870s, the Honourable A.F. Kinnaird could not be missed on the pitch. He wore cricket gear, a long red beard, and stood on his head when he won a match. And he did win a lot of matches, including nine English FA Cups, for the Wanderers and Old Etonians.

In the end, Scotland's FA clubs were bled dry of their best players and caved in to professionalism in 1893. By the end of the 19th century, paid teams both north and south of the border had time to devote to their sport. Gradually, their skills and tactics for the most part outshone those of many amateurs. In the end, apart from a few, these unpaid players just faded from the limelight.

CHAPTER SEVEN

ONLY THE BEST

"His [the footballer's] transfer papers have been prepared with all the detailed care and accuracy of a property."

Captain Philip Trevor, *The Badminton Magazine*, April 1897

PROFESSIONALISM LED TO the rise of the individual star who was "worth" a good wage. Clubs now wanted to scout for and "buy" these top players: a business that became the norm by the end of the 19th century. But this commercial venture didn't get by without a good deal of criticism.

SOCCER AND THE OPEN SORE

Surely clubs were only trying to get the best for the great game of football? So what could be the problem? Well, the slave trade was a recent and running scar on many peoples' consciences. Buying a human being — "a fit body" — seemed utterly distasteful and a dangerous move backwards. Slavery wasn't officially abolished in the Americas until Brazil finally let go of it in 1888. By this time, footballers were professional. They didn't just take expenses and sneak home "boot money" — they

World Player of the Year in 1996, 1997 and 2002, this piercing striker floats over the pitch, deceives defenders and scores goals from the tightest of angles.

Ronaldo Luiz Nazario de Lima

of a string of great clubs: PSV Eindhoven, Barcelona, Inter Milan, Real Madrid and Brazil (1976–)

He bagged eight goals for Brazil in the 2002 World Cup, earning him the Golden Boot award. But how would he have coped with a dominating defender such as Franz Beckenbauer?

SEE PAGE 70 FOR FRANZ BECKENBAUER

could earn a good wage. So for the many desperate British workers and workless, football was anything but enslavement — it was a tempting pot of gold. They certainly weren't going to argue against the professional game on moral grounds. Football was a beacon of hope — a way out of grinding poverty and endless toil. For many all over the world, it still is.

City splits

Everton's move to Goodison Park was forced on them by the landlord of their Anfield ground, who wanted to double the rent after they won the Cup in 1891. This same landlord, John Houlding, set up Liverpool Association Football Cup with a few of the Everton players. And here begins one of the many fierce and famous rivalries between clubs that share the same city, the same dreams, but not the same supporters.

CUP CLASHES — LEAGUE LEADERS

The English FA Cup Competition was a resounding success. Even in the early rounds, crowds soared in some instances to 10 000 people. But Cup fixtures ate into the menu of Saturday "friendly" matches. These had been the bread-and-butter games for players and spectators alike, but now clubs began to send their best teams to play in the highly prestigious Cup games. This meant that they had to field teams of unknown players for the Saturday games, which in any case were rather badly organised. Spectators were just not going to put up with these second-rate matches for much longer. Something had to be done.

It was a Scot, William McGregor, of Birmingham's Aston Villa Club, who found the solution. He set up a league of twelve clubs. The idea was that they would all play each other over the season both at home and away. The fixtures would take account of Cup-tie commitments so that the best players could be selected for both. Now why hadn't anyone thought of that before?

The new league teams were all situated north of Birmingham in the English Midlands. The southern sides ignored this progress and it was their loss, for by 1892 the football league had two divisions, and teams were raking in the money from huge attendances. The great game was gaining not just in pace, but also in rhythm, with the regular fixtures, loyal crowds, newspaper reports of matches, pin-up players, management movers-and-shakers, printed programmes and hawkers with barrows selling food for the spectators. A football culture was forming, and like a living organism, it swelled and multiplied across the land.

The whistle-blower

In 1875, Joseph Hudson from the English Midlands invented the famous "Acme Thunderer" football match whistle, which could be heard a mile away. Hudson's idea for the sound came when his violin dropped, letting out a piercing shrill as it shattered.

MODERNISING MOMENTS

GOAL POSTS	In 1863 the FA declared them to be 8 yards (7.32 metres) apart, and in 1875 a wooden crossbar replaced the tape strung between them.
THE BALL	All shapes and sizes were possible — and probable — until 1872. Then the FA insisted on a 27–29 inch round leather object. Most major teams agreed to use "Lillywhite's No. 5".
SHIN PADS	Sam Widdowson — what a hero! This Nottingham Forest player invented shin pads in 1874 — worn over the socks.
GOAL NETS	Scotland's John Brodie invented the "huge pocket" and Everton's Fred Geary scored the first netted goal in 1891. And who's this? Yes, Sam Widdowson, by this time a referee, was the man who called the goal, "Good!"
PENALTY KICKS	These sometimes devastating, sometimes joyful moments were invented by the Irish FA in 1890. Cruel.

PITCH MARKINGS By 1891, goal lines and touchlines were marked. So was a penalty-kicking line — 12 yards out from the goal and stretching right across the width of the pitch.

OFFSIDE From the 1870s until 1925, three defenders were needed between the attacker with the ball and the goal being attacked; after 1925 it was reduced to two.

FLOODLIGHTS In 1878, two noisy generators powered lights set on wooden towers at Sheffield United.

TURNSTILES By 1893 turnstiles were controlling the huge crowds at football stadiums. Birmingham City and Aston Villa still have their 1896 models.

A SOCCER SNAPSHOT

Imagine a stunning black-and-white panoramic photo of the 1879 English FA Cup Final. Aston Villa, in the lighter strip, is playing Everton in the darker one. Both teams are wearing comfortable knee-length, loose, white baggy shorts — "knickerbockers" as they were known then. Braces are probably holding these knickerbockers up, but they are hidden under the players' jerseys. Their feet are well-shod in leather football boots that are probably black but possibly brown, and legs are cosseted in long woolly socks, certainly with garters to hold them up.

Soccer's solid seventeen

By 1898, the new football code had seventeen rules – an organised framework. This gave the game huge opportunities for skill and competitiveness. The rules concerned: the pitch; ball size; the ball in play and out of it; throw-ins; goal kicks, corner-kicks; free-kicks; penalties; the number of players and what they wore; referees; linesmen; how play should start and when it should end; how a goal is scored; offside; fouls and bad behaviour.

The game is being hosted at the Crystal Palace ground in London — one of the main Cup Final venues. By now the goalposts have crossbars — but as yet, no nets. And the pitch is very wide, almost square and with white line-markings. There are rather strange markings in the penalty area. They remind me of two soap bubbles stuck together, one around each goal post. The goalkeeper will make goal kicks from whichever is closest to the ball when it goes out of play. And there are officials to make sure he gets it right. A linesman is standing to attention on one side, flag in hand, while the ref is poised, feet together, in the centre of the pitch. He's concentrating very hard on the ball and the players around it. The ball, by the way, is probably caramel-coloured and will get really soggy on this damp pitch.

It's the kick-off. The ball is close to the centre line and it's touch-and-go which side will run on to it first. Players have placed themselves in the formation typical of the times, and for decades to come: a 2–3–5. By this time, the offside rule will not allow the five forwards to string themselves out from the centre to the opposition's goalpost, waiting for a kick-through. There's no easy way to score. At each end of the pitch, the goalkeepers are perched on their lines, eyeing the movement of the ball like a pair of buzzards.

Football fashion

By the 1880s, football gear was well sorted and coordinated. Geo. G. Bussey's mail-order catalogue supplied: ear, shin and ankle guards; leather-and-rubber goalkeeper's gloves; Bussey's own patent Spring Athletic Belt; kit bags and even goal posts ... with special rates for clubs and schools.

The crowd is enormous — 66 000 people. But at this ground there's only three stands lined up along the side of the pitch. The central one is the tallest — the grandstand. But most spectators are standing, piled thirty to forty deep along sloping, grassy banks that surround the grounds. One man is standing on a stool so that he can get a better view.

Who's watching? Mostly men, all wearing hats — mainly bowlers and cloth caps — but there's also the rare woman's brimmed and ribboned boater. This headgear reveals a mixed crowd — perhaps of shopkeepers and clerks, skilled workers and labourers. The grandstand would have been reserved for posher people. All eyes in the crowd are dedicated to the game; they all seem passionate and completely focused. I can just feel the tension, the hype and the hope on that cold, smoggy afternoon in London. (And by the way, Aston Villa beat Everton 3–2. In spite of Everton's defeat, its superhero and Scottish international, John Bell, got man of the match for his two goals and fine dribbling.)

By this time, the Great Game has become one that we can all recognise. But were the British Isles alone in getting soccer sorted by the 20th century? Absolutely NOT.

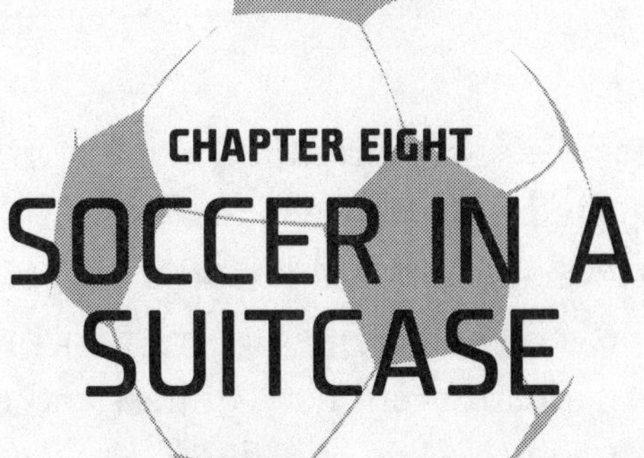

CHAPTER EIGHT

SOCCER IN A SUITCASE

"Other countries have their history. Uruguay has its football."

Ondino Viera: football guru and World Cup team manager

In London you'll see conkers scuffed along a path in a park. In West African Sahel it'll be calabashes kicked in the red dust. In southern Portugal it's outsized acorns skimmed around stony groves. It's an international habit, this kicking thing. And from the 19th century it was transformed into a sport and an industry across the globe because of Association Rules — soccer. Mostly, the game at this time was transported by football-crazed Britishers, unable to stop themselves from booting a ball (or rock or calabash) or organising other people to do the same.

BULLDOGS AND BULLDOZERS

By the end of the 19th century, the English had colonised about a third of the earth. The world map was splodged with pretty pink — the colour of the British Empire filling the area between the borders of many countries. All this was gained by aggressive trade, ceaseless exploration, menacing Christian missions, sly land contracts and, if all that failed, the gun. What this meant for a lot of Brits — from upper-class Commissioners to working-class butlers, engineers, architects, miners and merchants — was an awful lot of living abroad. Perhaps most important of all this — to football — were the railway officials and workers, who developed clusters of football clubs along the railway networks that crisscrossed the globe. And what went in their suitcases and toolbags? Yes, squashed footballs and well-used rules sheets.

Pockets of Brits ended up in the most far-out places: there were Welsh sheep farmers in Argentina's Patagonia, tin miners on Nigeria's Jos Plateau, and wheat farmers in outback Australia. Meanwhile, back in Britain, communities from all the corners of the earth settled in her heaving industrial cities, and sailors from all over the world ended up in ports around the British coastline. This continuous flow of people back-and-forth across the globe took football to the corners of the known world. But with only twenty miles of sea and sand banks between England and Europe, football fanned most quickly out among Britain's nearest neighbours. These are some of the ways that *fussball*, *futebol*, *voetbal* and *calcio* came about:

CLOSE CONTINENTAL CLUBS

FRANCE (1870s)	English sailors played football in the port of Le Havre and a club soon started.
SWEDEN (1870s)	Textile workers from Scotland took football to the industrial port of Gothenberg. Meanwhile in the capital Stockholm, British Embassy officials set up a soccer squad.
GERMANY (1875)	Oxford University students took a grand tour of German universities, taking the new Association Rules with them. German students took to football and straight away played by England's southern FA rules.
SWITZERLAND (1880s)	After attending public school, English lads often went to Swiss "finishing schools" to learn manners, deportment, French — and dancing. But they also belted a ball around. The Lausanne Football and Cricket Club, and others, were formed as a result.
ITALY (1893)	The first club formed was Genoa — just twenty-three years after the Kingdom of Italy was proclaimed.
SPAIN (1898)	British mining engineers working around Vizcaya set up the first Spanish club in the Basque region — the famous Atletico Bilbao.

Franz Beckenbauer was a defender with a twist. His timing, style and dominance made him the closest you'll get to a prima donna on the pitch. His position? Sweeper. Yes, sweeper. He revolutionised this underrated role and made it into a powerful, forward-pushing must-have for every team.

Franz Beckenbauer

Bayern Munich and West Germany (1945–)

With lightning runs from deep centre, he swelled the attack, shocking his opponents. Beckenbauer is the only player to have won the World Cup on the pitch and off it, as manager. But what would he have done with this legend … George Best?

SEE PAGE 78 FOR GEORGE BEST

CONFLICT ON THE CONTINENT

The pioneers of continental football weren't the great powerhouses of modern Europe — France, Germany, Italy, Spain and so on. In fact, even in the last half of the 19th century, some of these nations were only just born. Italy became a united country in 1870, with Rome as its capital. Germany got cobbled together in 1871, and there wasn't yet a Poland, Czech Republic or Hungary, because they all came under the whopping great Austro–Hungarian Empire. But at some point, these, Russia and other nations got the football bug. Then they set about organising football leagues and national associations. But with all their other distractions, none of them did it first. That prize went to the little kingdom of Denmark.

"WE ARE RED, WE ARE WHITE, WE ARE DANISH DYNAMITE"

Stuck out on a limb between the chilly North Sea and the Baltic, the Copenhagen Ball Club was formed in 1876. It was the first continental club and it was extremely excited about soccer. Cricket and rounders were fine, but these only took care of Denmark's short summers. By 1878, and in spite of frozen grass and long, inky nights, the club introduced football onto its menu, and into Europe. In 1889, Denmark became the first country outside the British Isles to handle the game in a truly organised way. In this year the Dansk Boldspil-Union — the Danish Football Association — was formed. And it wasn't long before Denmark won the Olympic gold medal in 1906 and silvers at both the 1908 and 1912 Olympic Games — losing to gold-medal winning Great Britain in both 1908 and 1912, and, incidentally, beating the bronze-medal winning Netherlands in both years too.

Stripey strips

Juve! Juve! Juventus! Students from D'Azeglio Lyceum in Turin set up this massive club in 1897. But how did they get their black and white shirts? Some say that England's Notts County gave them a set of their own red and black stripey shirts on a tour to Italy. The red stripe washed out pink. So a new set was sent out from Nottingham – this time, with white stripes – the closest colour they could get to pale pink.

Since then, Denmark has produced huge entertainment at club and international level, and many stars, including Peter Schmeichel and the Lauden brothers, Brian and Michael. Perhaps surprisingly, Denmark stubbornly resisted professionalism until 1978. This meant that many of its most talented players had to go abroad to find fame, fortune and to improve their game. But they always came back to represent their country — stronger and more competitive than ever. In August 2005 Denmark even triumphed over one of football's founding fathers. It thrashed England and its megastars — the likes of David Beckham — 4–0. It was David and Goliath, the might of the minnows. Football can conquer all predictions and no team is ever safe. What a mesmerising sport this is!

FOOTBALL AFAR

European football was getting sorted. But the rest of the world was coming along nicely, too.

ARGENTINA (1860s) British railway workers brought football to Argentina, and by 1865 British residents had formed the Buenos Aires Football Club.

CANADA (1876) The Carlton Cricket Club put together a winter football team, which later toured Britain.

BRAZIL (1884) The British Royal Navy docked in Brazil and passed on their football skills to the locals. I expect they wished they hadn't.

URUGUAY (1891) British railway workers set up the first sporting club in Uruguay, and a British professor at Montevideo University set up the first national team — paving the way for one of South America's most famous footballing nations.

MAGNIFICENT MILLER

In 1884, tender ten-year-old Charles Miller waved goodbye to his parents from a Brazilian quayside and set sail for England. Charles was the son of a senior British railway official in the city of Sao Paolo. Brazil had been a Portuguese colony until 1822, but 3000 Britons had wormed their way into Sao Paolo, creating their own little pocket of opportunists.

Mr Miller booked Charles into Bannisters School in southern England's port city of Southampton. Here, the young lad got stuck into Latin grammar, algebra, Shakespeare (who used a kicked ball as a metaphor for helplessness!) — and soccer. This last "study" became the young boy's undying passion. He learned to dribble the ball on Hampshire's short grass and hard chalkland, much loved by the sheep. He learned to swerve and dodge, feign, and then to charge ahead with the ball towards goal. Charles ended up playing for both Southampton Club and Hampshire County, as a skilled winger and striker. And then, in 1892, he joined the mighty Corinthians — that stoic amateur team of ex-public schoolboys who aimed to play the game with manners and skill.

Back in Brazil, they had set up the Sao Paolo Athletic Club (SPAC) in 1888. And when Charles returned to the city in 1894, his football gear and rule book came in handy. SPAC embraced his ideas for football with huge enthusiasm, and began to challenge other teams that were springing up all over the city. SPAC soon became the one to beat, winning the Sao Paolo championship easily in the first years of the city's competition.

SPAC played against English teams, too. These included Charles's old firms — Southampton and the Corinthians — who he had never forgotten. Charles knew that top competition was the best way of improving the club's game. The Corinthians toured in 1910, and when a new Sao Paolo football club needed a name, Charles naturally suggested "Corinthians". Brazil's Corinthians are still one of the nation's most famous premier sides and have developed some of the world's most exciting players.

Champion Charles left three major legacies: the drive for players to pursue the holy grail of excellence in football; good sportsmanship; and the excitement of his outstanding ball skills — especially his very own heel flick. This quick but deadly and difficult trick allows a player to change the direction of the ball — and the game. It was named the *Chaleiro* — after the famous Charles Miller.

CHAPTER NINE

MAKING IT HAPPEN

"Football has the incredible power to unite people for a peaceful gathering and shared enjoyment … there are 250 million registered players all over the world, which makes 250 million ambassadors for peace and fair play."

Sepp Blatter: FIFA President, accepting a peace prize in New York, 18 February 2004

THERE WAS A TERRIFIC thirst for international competition in the early days. The world was opening up through railway networks, bridges and roads that wormed their way through miles of solid rock. At this time it still took a few weeks to cross the Atlantic by ship, and double that to get to Australia and New Zealand. Footy festivals to far-off shores were more like expeditions. In spite of this, footballers fell over themselves to travel abroad to compete against the best players from other countries.

IT'S GOOD TO TALK

By the very end of the 19th century, communications between nations had got quicker and more reliable.

In 1899, the first wireless telegraph was sent across the English Channel, and in 1901 the first message was wired over 2000 miles of cable across the Atlantic, from England to the US. Postal services became faster and the world seemed to be shrinking. None of this was lost on Europe's leading national football organisers. It was now much easier to set up matches — to sort out venues, referees and slight differences in rules.

By the beginning of the 20th century, a few European international games had already taken place. But the clutch of continental countries with football associations wanted a lot more than the odd match. They wanted something deeper and more lasting: a body that would expand soccer on a global scale. They wanted an organisation that would ensure the quality of football, and regulate the behaviour of all those involved with the game.

SETTING UP SOCCER

If football was to conquer the world then it needed strong-minded, imaginative individuals to make it happen. And Carl Anton Wilhelm Hirschmann, the secretary of the Netherlands Football Association, was one of several great visionaries — he was passionate about football's future. Together with other European football associations, he wanted to create a worldwide football organisation, starting in his own corner of the globe.

Simply the Best?

George Best (1946–2005) of Northern Ireland, and Manchester United. Once named the best player of all time by Pelé, perhaps Best's rather brief career at the top didn't really merit that title. But his skills certainly did. He glided over the turf, swivelling and swerving and yet still kept the ball. His two-footed magic and sensitive passing bamboozled his opponents. But Best's personal life and intrusive media interest spoiled this one-man soccer show.

SEE PAGE 110 FOR MARTA VIEIRA DA SILVA

On Friday 25 November 2005, George Best died after a long battle with illness. Tributes poured in from all over the world. Football grounds across Britain pledged a minute's silence in his honour before their Saturday game. But at Best's beloved Old Trafford, and in true soccer spirit, a deafening round of applause erupted to acknowledge one of football's finest.

George Best

of Northern Ireland, and Manchester United (1946–2005)

A symbolic act for so many others who have given such pleasure to millions. Stars like Best certainly help keep the dream of soccer alive — a dream in which football lasts forever. The burden of success lies partly with the next generation of "bests", the Torres, the Messis, the Rooneys and Lodeiros … and of course, Marta …

Hirschmann was a continental European, but he desperately wanted to include the British football associations. He recognised them as the founding fathers of football. After all, they'd spread the game far and wide; they'd created soccer's seventeen rules. And they'd set up the International Football Association Board (IFAB) that monitored those rules — although "International" was rather stretching it; there were only four members: England, Ireland, Scotland and Wales. And what a stubborn, slow lot they were, too. Hirschmann had his work cut out trying to persuade them to come to the European party.

DIGGING IN THEIR HEELS

The secretary of the English FA said that he did like the idea of a federation of footballing nations. But were all these continental European football associations serious? Were they truly representative? Were they as proper as the English one? And of course, the English FA would have to consult the FA's Executive Committee, the IFAB, and the football associations of Ireland, Scotland and Wales. And … and … and … Well, if I was Hirschmann, I wouldn't have held my breath, but he actually did hold his. Robert Guerin, Secretary of the football wing of France's Union of Sports' Societies, wasn't as patient.

Guerin wanted to forge ahead without the British.

And although Hirschmann certainly wasn't out of the picture, it was Guerin who "picked up the ball and ran with it". He got together with the Secretary of the Belgian Football Association after a match on 1 May 1904, to discuss forming an international footballing body as soon as possible. He also wanted to talk about England's rather aggravating, snooty, snail-like behaviour. Both secretaries agreed that President Lord Kinnaird's English FA was stopping progress and would have to be left out for the time being.

Guerin wasted no time. He was a journalist on the famous French newspaper, *Le Matin*, and a confident writer. With great speed and skill he sent out persuasive invitations to football associations across Europe. He hoped so much that their representatives would turn up to the first meeting of the trail-blazing *Federation Internationale de Football Association* (FIFA). The following page shows who agreed to come …

FIRST FIFA – SMALL BUT PERFECTLY FORMED

BELGIUM	Union Belge des Societes de Sports (UBSSA)
DENMARK	Dansk Boldspil-Union (DBU)
FRANCE	Union des Societes Francaises de Sports Athletiques (USFSA)
THE NETHERLANDS	Nederlansche Voetbal Bond (NVB)
SPAIN	Spain was actually represented by Madrid FC, not a national football association — but this was agreed to by other Spanish football clubs
SWEDEN	Svenska Bollspells Forbundet (SFB)
SWITZERLAND	Association Suisse de Football (ASF)

MOVERS AND SHAKERS

These FIFA presidents have certainly kept international football alive. But sometimes their decisions and outbursts have caused a lot of controversy. Rather like some footballers — and some referees.

1904–1906	Robert Guerin of France
1906–1918	Daniel Woolfall of England
1921–1954	Jules Rimet of France
1954–1955	Rodolphe William Seeldrayers of Belgium
1955–1961	Arthur Drewry of England
1961–1974	Sir Stanley Rous of England
1974–1998	Dr Joao Havelange of France
1998–PRESENT	Joseph S. Blatter of Switzerland

MEETINGS OF MINDS

On 23 May 1904, the first FIFA Congress was held. Robert Guerin was elected President, with Hirschmann of the Netherlands and Switzerland's Victor E. Schneider as Vice Presidents. Under their leadership, the first FIFA statutes were set down. You will probably recognise the spirit of the statutes: the solidarity of FIFA's members and the firmness of its ideals. These two characteristics have held FIFA and international football together for over 100 years, through thick and thin.

FIFA'S FIRST FOOTSTEPS

FIFA pledged that it would only recognise national associations belonging to its organisation. There could be no rogue set-ups back home. Clubs and players could play for just one national association. If a player was suspended, all FIFA members had to recognise the suspension.

In a gesture of true goodwill, all FIFA's first pledges were made loose and temporary for a while. These were ideals rather than rules, they said, and set in sand rather than stone. FIFA didn't want them to be too rigid or seem too exclusive, as other nations might be put off joining them. And those first few FIFA members so wanted their organisation to be truly international.

This turned out to be a very smart move. Even on that first day, Germany's FA, the Deutscher

Fussball-Bund, hastily telegraphed FIFA saying that it wanted to belong. Later, on 14 April 1905, the English FA finally caved in and joined FIFA. They had kindly accepted that other countries' football associations were as good as their own. Soon after, Hungary, Italy and Austria all jumped aboard, just in time to attend the second FIFA Congress from 10–12 June 1905. Some of these new members had only just formed their own football associations. To them, belonging to FIFA was a huge boost of recognition — at home as well as abroad. Later, in 1906, Ireland, Scotland and Wales also sauntered into FIFA.

FIFA's finances

Who paid for FIFA? At first, each national football association had to cough up 50 French francs each year, but this wasn't enough and organisers and supporters of FIFA were always dipping into their own pockets. It was clear by the first World Cup of 1930 that FIFA had to take some profit from it. So they did – and they still do.

So now there were enough members to fulfil one of FIFA's main aims: to set up an international competition — and something on a grander scale than the rather scrappy Olympic football tournament of 1906 (won by Denmark), which was more like an exhibition contest. FIFA's first thoughts were that clubs representing each nation should compete. That there should be four groups, then semi-finals and a final. And that there should be a trophy. Well, most of that now sounds very familiar, but there were some hurdles along the way.

CASTING THE NET

FIFA has had its fair share of muddles across the years — its scandals, too. But its aim to unite the world through football has never faltered. FIFA's early teething problems — which resulted from a general lack of harmony — didn't stop its members from competing in two Olympic football tournaments. The 1908 and 1912 gold medals were both won by England, and the success of the competition put the heart back into FIFA. It was back on track, and the rest of the footballing world knew it. Nations outside Europe wanted to join — South Africa in 1909, Argentina and Chile in 1912, and the USA in 1913. These far-off football fanatics had gained

Football refinements

1904 In England, the Professional Footballers' Association (PFA) is formed to represent footballers' interests. It paves the way for other nations' footballers' unions.

1912 Goalkeepers can no longer handle the ball outside the penalty area. But they can kick it.

1913 When a free kick is taken, the opposing team must stand at least 10 yards from the ball.

confidence in FIFA as an organisation with truly open arms.

One of FIFA's greatest strengths was its acceptance of the very different football cultures of its member countries. Not just styles of play, venues and the like, but quite major variations in league systems, cup competitions and so on. FIFA operated on trust. Trust that whatever system a country had, it would try to abide by FIFA's rules, and that it would field the best teams it possibly could in international competition. Although, even in the early days, clubs exploded into a hissy fit when they were asked to release their best players for international matches!

BUYING THE SHIRT

There have been so many heroes on the football pitch — from Eusebio to Ronaldo, Socrates to Cruyff. But what about the boardroom? Who has a football shirt with "Hirschmann" emblazoned on the front? Or "Guerin"? Or, a later President of FIFA, the famous Jules Rimet? I mean, he even gave us the name of the World Cup trophy itself! So why not wear their names with pride? For there would be no global football as it exists today without these tireless troopers.

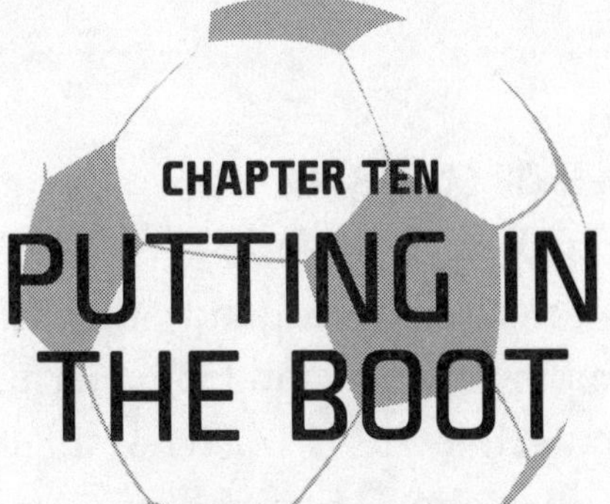

CHAPTER TEN

PUTTING IN THE BOOT

"If this can be termed the century of the common man, then soccer, of all sports, is surely his game … In a world haunted by the hydrogen and napalm bomb, the football field is a place where sanity and hope are still left unmolested."

Sir Stanley Rous (1895–1986): teacher, football referee, football administrator and President of FIFA 1967–74

THE SPIRIT OF FRIENDLY pride between nations crumbled to dust during the First World War — a bloody, barbaric conflict that lasted from 1914 to 1918, a conflict that sucked in soldiers from lands as far apart as Ireland and Australia. Nationalism and pride are such fragile feelings. They can inspire, but they can equally spiral into hatred. This is just what happened in Europe, where the conflict began. Nineteenth-century tussles led to niggling aggravations that turned into all-out war. Eight-and-a-half million people died. Bright young soldiers came back as broken old men — with no limbs, no sight, no hope. What happened to all those grand ideals that could be achieved through sports such as football? Could they endure such horror?

THE WONDER OF FOOTBALL

"Stille nacht, heilige nacht" — "Silent night, holy night". This peaceful carol and other wistful songs wafted across no-man's-land from German trenches on Christmas Eve in 1914. The singing soldiers hoisted candles above battered parapets; some on sticks — others on little Christmas trees. Slowly, weary fighters from both sides emerged from the stench of their frozen dugouts. They shook hands, warily at first. They talked: for some, it was just the language of smiles and kind gestures.

On Christmas Day, small gifts were exchanged — whatever meagre treats the soldiers had. Maybe some chocolate or tobacco; beer or schnapps; buttons or badges — and little tins of beef. And what happened next can only show the power of "the Beautiful Game" and the possibilities it inspires for bridging even cosmic divides such as world wars. A few soldiers had managed to stuff a soccer ball into their kit bags. Here and there, up and down hundreds of miles of stinking, rat-ridden trenches, enemies played friendly games of football. Many of their friends and foes lay dead all around them. Here is one soldier's true soccer tale …

LIEUTENANT NIEMANN'S CHRISTMAS SURPRISE

On Christmas Day in 1914, Germany's 133rd Royal Saxon Regiment faced the Scottish Seaforth Highlanders along the Western Front on the

French–Belgian border. Christmas Eve had been quiet, apart from simple festive celebrations — and painful, silent yearnings for home. But a German officer, Lieutenant Johannes Niemann was still keeping watch. He was nervous and his hearing was acute; he picked up a strange buzz. It was coming from outside the trenches. The Lieutenant snatched his binoculars and peered through them in horror and amazement. Soldiers were crisscrossing the 100 yards of barbed wire and slush — to talk, laugh, and shake each others' frost-bitten hands. Who on earth had given his soldiers permission to do THAT? Well, no-one. And no-one had agreed to the soccer game that followed. The Lieutenant's surprise turned to delight as a Scot magicked a football from the British trenches. The Lieutenant reported:

> A real football match got underway. The Scots marked their goal mouth with their strange caps and we did the same with ours. It was far from easy to play on the frozen ground, but we continued, keeping rigorously to the rules, despite the fact that it only lasted an hour and that we had no referee. A great many passes went wide, but all the amateur footballers, although they must have been very tired, played with enthusiasm.

A truly remarkable, epic match. But also short-lived. The next day was 26th December: the friends became soldiers again. They returned to their own trenches, and these same men who had only aimed a ball at goal the day before, now aimed weapons of war at each other, in deadly combat.

So what happened to football outside the trenches? Well, it wasn't entirely blown away. Internationals were played during the conflict, even on the war-torn mainland of Europe. Neutral territories were found to stage these very important games; without them it would have been so much harder for FIFA to get back to the table when war was over. In fact, it would have been almost impossible if it hadn't been for one remarkable man.

A double whammy
The Great War was followed by the 'flu epidemic of 1918. This took even more lives than the war itself. Many football stars whose faces had smiled from posters and cigarette cards, playing cards and football annuals now lay buried – most in far-off fields. Countless teams on all sides had lost more than half of their squad.

HIRSCHMANN THE HERO

Carl Anton Wilhelm Hirschmann — Secretary of the Netherlands Football Association, and Honorary Secretary of FIFA — was the man who had so generously opened his arms to the grumbling Brits in FIFA's early days. Now he made it his mission to keep alive the dream of FIFA during that terrible war. Communications between FIFA's members were almost impossible at this time — politically, emotionally and physically. Many parts of Europe were just lakes of blood and mud. Rail tracks, roads, bridges and tunnels were ruined. And in any case, many FIFA members weren't in the mood for cuddling up to each other.

But Hirschmann never gave up. From his offices in Amsterdam he ran FIFA's Secretariat, in his own time and with his own money. He wrote letters, lots of them, to other FIFA members — and he kept the channels of communication open throughout the war and beyond. After the war, Hirschmann stepped up his contact with other football associations. In this, he was encouraged by the President of the French Football Association, Jules Rimet.

PICKING UP THE PIECES

The war ended in 1918 and Hirschmann set up a FIFA Congress in 1919. But it was too soon. War wounds were still very raw. British football associations in particular were in no mood to share a table with some of their recent enemies. But in 1920, a more successful FIFA congress took place in Antwerp, although there were still some empty chairs. Jules Rimet was elected Chairman and all the missing members had to agree to all the new positions in the organisation through a postal vote. However, this was the first and last time that members could sit at home and still have their say. After the 1920 meeting, FIFA stuck to a strict policy of "show up or shut up". Sometimes you have to be cruel to be kind — and FIFA's firmness carried them through yet another world war in 1939.

CASTING A WIDER NET

The First World War was focused in Europe, but it also affected the far corners of the globe. Many of the warring nations had territories overseas. Remember the British Empire? Well, there was a French one, too — with huge tracts of land in Africa. Belgium also controlled part of Central Africa's Congo and the Netherlands had long-standing ties with Dutch East Indies (which includes modern-day Indonesia). Portugal held Angola and Mozambique, and still maintained transatlantic trade links with its old colony, Brazil. Before the war, Germany controlled East Africa's Tanganyika (now Tanzania) and South West Africa (Namibia). Fighting took place here, too — and in other, scattered parts of the world. Soldiers from the far reaches of the British Empire also came to Europe to fight for the country that ruled them. The famous ANZACs sailed half-way round the world from Australia and New Zealand to fight for Britain, their "Mother Country".

After the war, Germany had to give up its colonial territories. Through the new international League of Nations, Britain was now allowed to administer German colonies in Africa. So she sent her civil servants to Tanganyika and South West Africa. And yes, they probably stuffed footballs into their briefcases!

WHICH WAY INTERNATIONAL COMPETITION?

Some time before the First World War, FIFA hadn't really been in a position to take charge of the first few Olympic football competitions. There were some awkward differences between Olympic organisers and the many football associations. For one thing, the Olympic Games were staunchly amateur, whereas football had all the modern trappings of professionalism — both in terms of money and razzamatazz. But on the eve of war, at the 1914 FIFA Congress in Christiania, members agreed that their sporting aims fitted with those of the Olympic movement. Still, nothing could be done to set up an Olympic soccer competition until

---

Goals galore

Uruguay's results at the 1920 Antwerp Olympics were phenomenal: 7–0 against Yugoslavia; 3–0 against the US; 5–1 against France; and 2–1 against the Netherlands. Uruguay then beat Switzerland in the final, 3–0, and 60 000 people flocked to watch the game.

---

the 1920 Games in Antwerp, where Belgium won the soccer Gold. But it was at the Paris Olympic Games of 1924 where football landed with a big, glorious explosion of talent.

Twenty-four nations took part, including America and Uruguay. What an exciting prospect! Uruguay might as well have been Uranus for all anyone knew about it. The spectators were enthralled — South American soccer attracted them like bees to a honeypot.

The Uruguayans didn't disappoint. Their game was based on discipline and skill. On possession, possession and possession — followed by sharp, accurate forward passing. Possession meant excellent ball skills and forward passing — perfect positioning, timing and targeting. This tight package showed that the Uruguayans had trained, trained and trained. Football standards had suddenly hit the stars, and the Uruguayans' long journey was forgotten in their triumph. Back home, the capital Montevideo went mad.

Uruguay followed their first Olympic Gold in 1924 with another in 1928. She was on a roll. Now this small nation wanted the biggest prize of all — to host the first World Cup in Montevideo. What a triumph this would be! This little nation squashed between mighty Brazil to the east and Argentina to the west was going to show them all how it should be done.

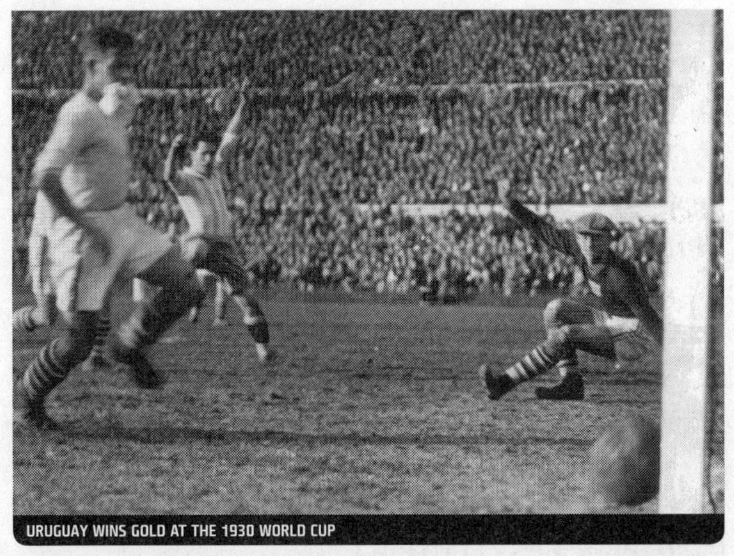
URUGUAY WINS GOLD AT THE 1930 WORLD CUP

FIRST WORLD CUP FURY

Montevideo was not a popular choice among FIFA's European members. Firstly, it was half a world away from Europe, where most FIFA members lived, and Europe was in the middle of a long economic depression. Money was tight and European football associations were reluctant to splash out on tickets to South America. Not only that, clubs back home complained that they needed their best players. They just weren't prepared to let them go for two whole months. (Pretty much the same argument that we hear today!)

So who was going to save the face of FIFA in Europe? Just four nations: France, Belgium, Yugoslavia and Romania refused to let FIFA down. They made a huge effort and took the long journey to Montevideo. And was it worth it? Of course! And did anyone miss the teams that wouldn't take part? Of course not! And who won the Cup? Uruguay!

The World Cup was voted a great success at the next FIFA Congress in Budapest. The support in Montevideo had been tremendous. Money poured into the game. But Uruguay was still stinging from Europe's poor participation in Montevideo, and she refused to defend her title in Italy at the next World Cup. Since then, sulking and tantrums have been a part of football too.

MORE WAR, LESS FOOTBALL

During the 1930s unease was spreading across Europe and the world. Germany was rearming under Adolph Hitler, and to the east, Japan was threatening China. The Paris FIFA Congress of 1938 was an uninspired event, and only a year later came the Second World War — one which ended in atomic bombs and a huge political crack in Europe, between communist and non-communist countries.

ENGLAND'S NAZI SALUTE ALONGSIDE THE GERMANS, 1938

During this second "war to end all wars" it's hard to find any record of friendly football matches across no-man's-land. It was a very different war fought in a very different way, and with new weapons and tactics. This time, even more countries took part in the fighting. Many were still under colonial rule. Soldiers were fighting against evils that they recognised — against fascism and dictatorship, racism and prejudice. They recognised them because many had suffered from them under their colonial masters.

After the Second World War, soldiers from the colonies decided that they would fight hard to gain freedom from their colonial rulers. So new, independent nations emerged from the gloom of repression. Freedom brought few solutions to the difficult financial positions of these ex-colonies, but a breath of fresh air blew into football. A new pool of talent and enthusiasm rocked the sleepiness of football's cosy world. The game expanded rapidly among African nations, who quickly set up their own football associations — and who also joined FIFA as soon as they could.

FIFA got its act together with great speed at the end of the conflict. The FIFA Congress resumed in Luxembourg in 1946, and thirty-four national organisations were represented. This year was also Jules Rimet's 25th year as President of FIFA — his jubilee. The World Cup was now to be called the Jules Rimet Cup. What a well-deserved honour!

WHAT HAPPENED AT THE WORLD CUPS?

1930 (held in Uruguay) Uruguay beat Argentina 4–2.

1934 (held in Italy) Italy defeated Czechoslovakia 2–1. This was the first World Cup to be broadcast on the radio.

1938 (held in France) Italy beat Hungary 4–2. Jules Rimet finally held the World Cup on his home turf, but it was by no means a full World Cup contingent: Argentina and Uruguay boycotted the competition, and Austria qualified but withdrew, as the country had been annexed by Germany.

1942 The Second World War got in the way of this one — and the next.

1950 (held in Brazil) To their frustration, Brazil lost to Uruguay 2–1.

1954 (held in Switzerland) West Germany (split at this time from Communist East Germany) beat Hungary 3–2.

1958 (held in Sweden) Brazil beat Sweden 5–2.

1962 (held in Chile) Brazil wins over Czechoslovakia (now the separate Czech Republic and the Republic of Slovakia) 3–1.

1966 (held in England) England defeats West Germany 4–2 — and English football has struggled to live up to this win ever since.

1970 (held in Mexico) Brazil beat Italy 4–2.

1974 (held in West Germany) West Germany defeated Holland 2–1.

1978 (held in Argentina) Holland lost again — this time to Argentina 3–1.

1982 (held in Spain) Italy beat West Germany 3–1.

1986 (held in Mexico) It's Argentina again — defeating West Germany 1–0. On the way, football legend Diego Maradona fists the ball into the goal in the quarter finals against England. That goal is now famously referred to as "the hand of God".

1990 (held in Italy) Sweet revenge! West Germany beats Argentina 1–0.

1994 (held in United States) It's a goalless draw between Brazil and Italy; Brazil wins on penalties.

1998 (held in France) France defeats Brazil 3–0.

2002 (held in Korea/Japan) Brazil wins over a politically united Germany 2–0.

2006 (held in Germany) Promoted as the "cuddly games", it was Italy that felt the cosy warmth of winning. They beat France 5–3 in a tense penalty shootout for their fourth World Cup win. Germany was a good host, but their reputation was tarnished by a cruel hoax that they had bribed their way into holding the event during the 2000 selection.

2010 (to be held in South Africa). The first African venue of all time. But will an African country win? What about the young, talented team from Ghana? They were defeated by a dazzling Egypt 1–0 in the 2010 Africa Cup Final but were missing some major players. So who knows? What we do know is that Ireland will be watching the final from their armchairs. Their fairytale ended at the qualifying stage through a goal scored against them by another handball — this time attached to the arm of France's Thierry Henri. So we can look forward to watching France in South Africa. Hands up all those who want them to win.

WINNING WAYS

All is not lost if the World Cup goes to another team. Yours could win the FIFA Fair Play Award or the Most Entertaining Team Award. Your players could pick up the Golden Boot for scoring the most goals, the Golden Ball Award for Best Player (or Silver for second best, Bronze for third), and your goalie could get the Yashin Award, named after the famous Russian goalkeeper, Lev Yashin.

CHAPTER ELEVEN

THE WORLD OF WOMEN'S FOOTBALL

"I like my women to be feminine, not sliding into tackles and covered in mud."

Brian Clough (1935–2004) Manager of Nottingham Forest and Derby County

FOR MUCH OF THE 19th century women and football weren't seriously engaged. Only the odd — actually, very odd — mention of women and football surfaces in the history books. Like the poor wife of the ball manufacturer, H.J. Lindon. In the 1850s she supposedly blew up so many pigs' bladders that her lungs gave out. Sadly, she died as a result, and H.J. Lindon went on to help develop the rubber inner tube. Like footballs, things for women could only get better.

GIRLS CAN DO ANYTHING

By the 1890s, women had been practising football in the park for a couple of decades. It was time to brave the blokes' baying and barracking. A proper match was scheduled in Glasgow in 1892, and another in

England in 1895. The one in England was organised by the newly formed British Ladies' Football Club. This clash was an all-London derby between North and South.

Miss Nettie J. Honeyball (her real name), the Club's secretary and captain, organised a good deal of promotion. And it worked. About 10 000 spectators turned up and a lot of gate money was taken. Who wouldn't want to watch two teams of defiant women footballers? Dressed in stiff ballooning blouses and bloomers, and strapping shin guards, these brave women ignored the frowns and sulks of the English Football Association and of course, the press.

Nettie Honeyball had dreamed she could "prove to the world that women are not 'the ornamental and useless' creatures men have pictured". In Great Britain, women's football flew high at some points, and then sunk really low. In recent decades women's soccer has taken off big time — especially in the United States. Yes, things brighten up for women later on. In fact, they get quite star-spangled.

WOMEN AT WAR — AND AT PLAY

During both world wars, women filled the holes in society left by the men who were away fighting. They worked in all sorts of tough jobs, in factories and in mines, and they performed their tasks extremely well. In their spare time, these women got together to raise money for wounded, shocked soldiers; for hospitals; and for poor, orphaned children. And what better way to do this than to entertain people with a really attractive, passionate and skilful game of football?

In 1917 the talented women from Dick Kerr's weapons' factory took to the pitch for the first time, and they were a resounding success. During and after the war they toured Britain, pulling in huge crowds. But they weren't content to leave it at that. They beat a women's team in France and, wait for it … a men's team in the United States! More than this, they encouraged other women's teams. They raised the profile of football as a whole, and they raised more than £70 000 for good causes — that's about £14 million in today's money.

Alice Barlow – barred from football

Alice Barlow played right half in Dick Kerr's Ladies. Her opinion of the LFA's 1921 decision? "We could only put it down to jealousy. We were more popular than the men and our bigger gates were for charity. I don't swear so I can't tell you what some of the team said … it was sad, because they'd been such happy times."

And then … bang! In 1921 the English Football Association barred women's teams from all grounds affiliated to them. That's all the big ones — the ones with terraces, facilities and the buzz. Their reasons?

Well, they said they were worried that women might get "hurt" by playing football. Very thoughtful, eh? What else? Oh, yes: did all that gate and programme money really go to charity? Now this was just a nasty slur. But how many excuses can you make up, really? So, with no major venues available to them, and no support from football's major organisers, women's games and teams fizzled out. Dick Kerr's Ladies were left to play on far-out, muddy fields. But first they organised a procession on a float to Blackpool — and the float was piled high with all their magnificent trophies.

The English Football Association kindly allowed women's football back onto its grounds in 1969. But it was only in 1993 that the organisation took the women's game under its wing and began to put some money into it.

It is taking a long time for English club teams to reach the levels of those in the rest of Europe. It has long been held back by a lack of cash. But at last the women's game is receiving central funding from the English Football Association. As the national team now lies eighth in the world rankings this investment is well deserved. They must really admire support structures of other nations though, such as Sweden.

QUEEN OF CONTINENTAL CLUBS

Sweden's Umeå IK is a women's league club well ahead of the game. By encouraging different styles and skills from international stars such as Brazil's Marta and Elaine, Umeå IK has won the UEFA (Union of European Football Associations) Women's Championship League in 2003 and 2004, were runners up in 2002, 2007 and 2008 and have reached the quarter finals for the 2009/2010 season. At home in Sweden, they're top of the tree — winning their premier league nearly every year in the 21st century! But even they would admit that out of all European national squads, Germany still glitters the brightest. It wasn't always like that though.

Michelle, football belle

Michelle Akers (1966–) is one of the most successful US women soccer players of all time. As a stunning centre-forward she won the Golden Boot award at the 1991 Women's World Cup — and was on the 1999 winning team, too. Akers is the second all-time super-scorer behind the legendary Mia Hamm. With role models like these, women's soccer in the US is bound to shine.

TOO FRAIL FOR FOOTBALL

Yes, German women were far too frail for football. So said the Deutscher Fussball-Bund (DFB) — the German Football Association of West Germany (Germany has been united with the East since 1991).

And when did the DFB pronounce this? Surely a hundred years ago or more? No, as recently as 1955 — when the great Pelé was still playing at junior level. What the DFB actually said was that women were so frail that they would not be able to take part in the sport without hurting themselves.

The years rolled by — but women's football was stuck in a rut. Finally in 1970, women were allowed to play — but only in warm weather. And with no studs on their football boots ... and the matches were shorter than the men's. Not until a proud performance by Germany's women in the 1989 European Competition for Women's Football did the light dawn for DFB. Finally, in 1990 they allowed women their own Bundesliga.

Now, over half a million women in Germany play organised football. They vastly overshadow other European nations, especially the "home" of football, Britain. Germany's national team has won the FIFA Women's World Cup in 2003 and 2007 and has ranked in the world's top three for the last ten years. The team's captain, Birgit Prinz, has been named FIFA's World Champion of the Year three times and is the top goal-scorer in the Women's World Cup. Now how frail is that? For other parts of the world, Germany is a great example. No more so than in Africa and Asia.

GALZ! GALZ! GALZ!

In Africa the popularity of soccer is exploding. With stars like Didier Drogba, Samuel Eto'o and Michael Essien, African players are sought-after by top football clubs throughout Europe. But what about the women? Many play, but have been frustrated by a lack of input from their own national sports' authorities — and world organisations, too. But all that is changing.

Namibia, a country of desert and savannah in Africa's south-west corner, just loves its footy. From the nation's population of just over 2 million, 3 700 women in six different leagues play some serious football. Since 2008 FIFA, UNICEF and nearby South Africa's Sports' Coaches Outreach (SCORE) organisation have invested in a "Galz and Goals" programme. It is designed to develop the potential of Namibia's Under-15 girls. The coaching courses in technical, tactical and organisational skills in Namibia's women's football have already paid off. In 2009, an Under-14 team played in the Norway Cup and there are plans for Namibian representation in the Hessequa Cup in South Africa in 2010. This young tournament runs alongside the World Cup and is open to amateur and youth teams.

KICKING ACROSS THE INDIAN OCEAN

Let us whizz eastward to India and Pakistan where women have played football since the 19th century.

As in many other parts of the world, the game here has lacked investment, organisation and publicity. In some regions it has also faced social and cultural obstacles. Challenges like these have made football associations fearful or perhaps just reluctant to develop the game at the mass grassroots level.

In Pakistan, the first public women's match was only played as recently as 2004. Encouraged by the response, the Pakistan Football Federation (PFF) held the first National Women's Soccer Championship in 2005. Eight teams took part that year, then twelve in 2006, rising to fourteen in 2007.

By 2008, the PFF realised that it had to tackle one of the biggest problems. Most of the teams were from posh city areas. The players were daughters of wealthy, educated people. Less privileged players were hard to find. The PFF decided that it could encourage mass grassroots support by reducing its registration fees. But what about all the other obstacles — the social and cultural? The women's game could no longer ignore them after the 2007 Fourth FIFA Women's Football Symposium in Shanghai, where the headline issue was "Overcoming Cultural Barriers".

This focus has encouraged many involved in football in Pakistan to speak out. They believe strongly that football workshops in poor city and rural areas will be more long-lasting than cheap registration. So, too, will a higher profile for women's football in the media, and properly trained women organisers, coaches and referees. This is true development.

SOCCER SOLIDARITY

A strong start was made in 2007 when FIFA and the PFF invited Monika Staab to coach in a six-week football camp and select a national squad. Just the right person, for Staab played in Frankfurt, Germany, in the 1970s — remember the DFB and their attitude to women footballers? So she knew quite a bit about cultural barriers!

Monika Staab's time in Pakistan was short but she was deeply impressed by the enthusiasm of the footballers and all those who supported them, both men and women. At an international tournament at the end of her stay, Staab said, "Four thousand spectators, twenty journalists and ten teams of reporters filming — I never had that in Frankfurt!"

International tournaments have given Pakistan's women players and the PFF examples of good practice from over the border into Afghanistan, and beyond, to Iran. These two nations were invited by the PFF to send a team to Pakistan's National Women's Soccer Federation Championship. In 2007 Afghanistan took home the silver medal. In 2009 the Iranian team won, scoring a staggering 68 goals in just five matches. They must be getting it right.

Pelé With Skirts

That's the nickname of Brazil's Marta Vieira da Silva. Not sure how it should be taken really, but it does provide a great image of Marta's skill, flair and success with the ball. Born in 1986, this young forward has been awarded FIFA Women's Player of the Year in 2006, 2007, 2008 and 2009. Not surprising as she scored 111 goals in 103 appearances for the Swedish team, Umeå IK. She was awarded the Golden Boot as the top scorer in the 2007 Women's World Cup, and the Golden Ball as the best player. Marta is now back in Brazil on loan to Santos after a stunning spell at Los Angeles Sol.

It's no surprise that Marta is the first woman player to be asked to imprint her boots in cement at the famous Estadio do Maracana. And Marta doesn't take this fame lightly. In 2009,

Marta Vieira da Silva

of Santos and Brazil (1986–)

when she was named FIFA Player of the Year for the fourth time in Zurich, Marta said it was "a landmark in my career and in my life." Now that's the power of football for you!

SOCCER IN THE STATES

Across the Atlantic, women in the United States had taken to sport in a big way. Cycling had been all the rage in the late 19th century, but it was almost impossible to turn the pedals in a long skirt and fussy petticoat. And you couldn't ride side-saddle! So large, comfortable bloomer-like trousers were designed to separate women's legs but still protect their modesty. Now they could ride bikes, run races — and play football.

Women's professional sport in America still lagged behind men's, as it did almost everywhere else (and still does). But professional women's football had a slightly better start and is well developed today. These days, women command star-spangled wages, transfer fees and commercial endorsements. They attract massive crowds of both men and women. And the game is used to encourage youngsters into activities of all kinds — with true sporting spirit.

SUPER STATES

In 1991 the US women's team won the very first Women's World Cup in Guangzhou, China, defeating the Norwegians 2–1. China, the Nordic countries such as Norway and Germany, and South American nations all competed fiercely for the Cup. And now, the women's game is developing at breakneck speed in Africa's soccer-mad nations, too.

WOMEN'S WORLD CUP FINALS

1991 (held in China) United States beat Norway 2–1.

1995 (held in Sweden) Norway beat Germany 2–0.

1999 (held in the US) The score was 0–0 but the United States beat China in a penalty shoot out, after a fruitless sudden death extra time.

2003 (held in the US) Germany beat Sweden 2–1 by a golden goal in a sudden death extra time.

2007 ((held in China) Shocks rippled through this sparkling tournament. Germany thrashed Argentina 11–0 in the opening match and Brazil stunned the US with a 4–0 win in the semi-final. The US had remained unbeaten for 51 games! A memorable final was set up between Germany and Brazil. But in spite of the skill and speed of Brazil's Marta and Mayon, Germany's calm consistency and sound tactics won the day. They beat Brazil 2–0, raised the Cup and looked forward to hosting the next fab final.

2011 (to be held in Germany) Qualifying matches for 2011 began on 19 September 2009 and will end on 25 August 2010. The strength of the women's game is clearly shown by the need for eight qualifying groups. And countries spanning the circumference of the world are taking part — from the tiny Mediterranean island of Malta to the mighty US.

It looks like the US has had most of the luck hosting the Women's World Cup. In fact, China was set to stage it in 2003. But the country was hit by the SARS virus and the tournament was off. Or was it? In the true spirit of the game, the US stepped in. China was still allowed direct entry to the competition as "host" nation, and was given the right to hold the 2007 Women's World Cup as compensation. Nothing was going to stop the Women's World Cup or the solidarity of its women's footballing nations.

WORLD CLASS WOMEN

Sen Han of China, and both Mia Hamm and Michelle Akers of the US, were all chosen by Pelé in his Top 125 Players of All Time. In 2000, Michelle Akers was named Miss Soccer of the Century by FIFA.

WORLD-CLASS WOMEN REFEREES

Bentla D'Coth was a very talented left-winger. She played for India in many internationals, including three Asian championships. But her footballing career didn't stop when she hung up her boots. Bentla soared to new heights as a referee. After taking charge of over 20 internationals, FIFA selected her for the 2004 Athens Olympics.

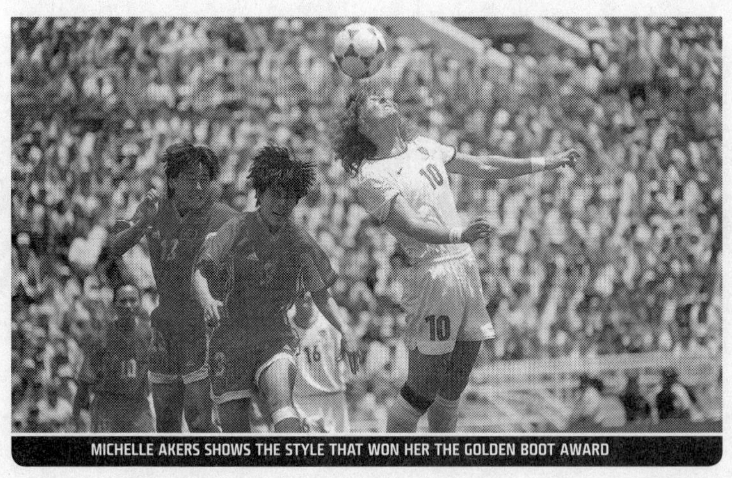

MICHELLE AKERS SHOWS THE STYLE THAT WON HER THE GOLDEN BOOT AWARD

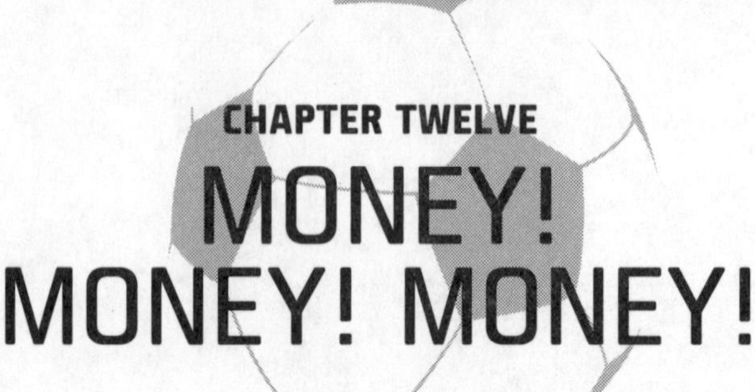

CHAPTER TWELVE

MONEY! MONEY! MONEY!

"I've told the players we need to win so that I can have the cash to buy some new ones."

Chris Turner, 1992, just before his Peterborough side played a League Cup quarter final match

THIS CRUSHING MESSAGE lays bare the chicken-and-egg nature of football finance. It goes like this. You need to win to get megabucks from corporate sponsorship and TV broadcasting rights. But you need good players in order to win. And to get good players you need megabucks from sponsorship and broadcasting rights. Or do you?

Is it really true that expensive individual players can raise a club to great heights on their own? Whatever happened to football as a team game? In the current economic downturn some clubs aren't buying and selling players as often. They are working with the players they have and are paying more attention to teamwork. The result? Subtle tactics, greater awareness of team positioning and more flexibility.

Perhaps you don't agree, for there are as many opinions on football as there are blades of grass on the pitch. And there are still scores of footballers whose fees are breaking the bank. How did they get to be so rich and famous?

THE CULT OF THE CIGARETTE CARD

As we know, footballers have been paid to play the great game for well over 100 years ago. The very best players became famous through national newspaper reports — and products. The first effective example of these was the cigarette card.

In England in 1896, the first series of cards featuring football players was produced. And the puffing public was hooked — on the cigarettes, the cards ... and the players.

Nowadays, as the health risks of smoking are so enormous, cigarette advertising in sport is banned in many countries. While the idea of associating smoking with playing sport seems

---

Collecting cards

In 1871 the US cigarette manufacturer Allen and Ginter thought of putting a piece of card into every box of cigarettes to protect them.
A couple of years later, to add a bit of interest, these "stiffeners" were printed with a picture.
By 1876 smokers could collect a whole series of fascinating cards with facts as well as pictures.
The whole point was to encourage people to collect the series – and stick to the same brand of cigarette.

---

outrageous now, at the time the gimmick was very effective in promoting players. The faces and facts of famous footballers spread across the nation.

When card collecting reached its peak in the 1920s and 1930s, footballers' celebrity status was secured forever. Cigarette manufacturers were by this time sponsoring the best footballers, too. Other products such as men's cosmetics jumped onto the bandwagon. Since then, all over the world, every kind of product you can imagine, from banks and builders to drinks and refrigerators, has been linked to top class football players.

SPOILT SPORTSMEN?

By the 1950s sponsorship income was a major boost to footballers' rather poor pay — especially in England. The great Sir Stanley Matthews managed to pocket £20 a week from the Cooperative Society while other players had to take on extra work to help pay the bills. Legendary Tom Finney of Preston North End worked as a plumber, while Billy Liddell took on a part-time job as an accountant.

In 1952 Tom Finney was offered £10 000 pounds as a personal payment by Italy's Palermo club. But Preston wanted a staggering £50 000 in transfer fees — a record at that time. So Tom Finney stayed at Preston. At times he would have looked longingly at clubs across the seas, and footballers who gained from them. Footballers such as Zoltán Czibor.

THE HUNGARIAN HURRICANE

Zoltán was a star member of Hungary's famous Magical Magyar national side in the 1950s. A side that thrashed England 7–1 in 1954. Hungary at that time was a member of the Communist Bloc — a group of socialist countries dominated by the powerful USSR. Under the communists, top players became heroes and were treated well. But opportunities for financial gain were few.

All this changed for Zoltán Czibor after the failed Hungarian Uprising against communism in 1956. The revolt was put down with such brutality that Zoltán knew his life and his career would be even more limited than before. So after playing for the Hungarian club, Honved, in the European Cup (and failing) in Brussels, he stayed on in non-communist Europe.

So began a rewarding football career outside the Bloc. In Europe, star players were paid star salaries and transfer fees. Zoltán played for FC Barcelona and then for RCD Espanol, FC Basel, FK Austria Wien and finally went to Canada, where he ended his career at Primo Hamilton. He made a good life for himself and his family, as so many great footballers do today.

WHO'S TOP DOLLAR NOW?

So which famous footballers are crying (loudest) all the way to the bank? It could be Zlatan Ibrahimovic and Kaka who in 2010 both received a cool £160 000 a week to play for Inter Milan. They're followed closely by Lionel Messi of Barcelona on £156 000. Chelsea's John Terry and Frank Lampard are on £140 000. Messi's team mates Samuel Eto'o and Thierry Henri are hot on their heels at £120 000. Cristiano Ronaldo of Real Madrid is in the same bracket and will find himself much better off now that he is no longer paying UK tax rates!

While the first two stars on this list get paid the most by their clubs they are still not necessarily the greatest earners. With sponsorship deals, some say that Cristiano Ronaldo and Frank Lampard are the top earners. Or nearly. Even in the twilight of his career, David Beckham is probably still beating the lot. In 2010 he was on loan from LA Galaxy to AC Milan, and still on a stellar salary. With stunning sponsorship deals from Asia and his own thriving Footwork Productions Company, David Beckham is definitely the financial whizkid of the football world.

But all this money has made some players spoilt and peevish. In 2006, England's Ashley Cole was dubbed Cashley Cole when he complained that his contract renewal with Arsenal offered a mere £55 000 per week instead of the "promised" £60 000. Poor guy — thank goodness he ended up bagging £120 000 with Chelsea.

Top soccer salaries sound like a dream. But they

have been breaking some clubs' finances and their fans hearts over the last ten years. How do collapsing clubs cope?

CLUBS IN CRISIS

Top clubs can still be faced with top troubles. Portsmouth, southern England's beloved "Pompey", first struck a ball in 1898. But this club's proud history is now overshadowed by money matters. It is buried in debt and has slumped into "Administration" (it is no longer allowed to control its own finances). The team, though, is focusing on its footy and continues to win. In March 2010 it reached the semi-finals of the English FA Cup.

And what about mighty Manchester United? Yes, this colossal club owes a palm-sweating billion dollars. Prices of tickets and club merchandise have climbed. The fans are foaming at the mouth and want the club's owners, the Glazer Brothers from the United States, OUT. A group of heavyweights in the financial world have entered the battle for their proud club. Known as the "Red Knights", these financial wannabe saviours are fronted by Goldman Sachs bank's chief economist, Jim O'Neill. The "Knights" are putting on their armour, climbing into the saddle and charging at the Glazers. Will they succeed? Not a chance — they're "Not For Sale", according to United's Chief Executive, David Gill. We shall see.

What we do know is that in Britain, debts have to paid back — often with huge interest. Banks won't bail them out, either. But what about football's collapsing clubs in other parts of the world?

WIPING THE SLATE CLEAN

In Spain, many famous clubs have owed serious amounts of money. Barcelona and Real Madrid were on top — not only for their football but also their debt levels. And were they bothered? Probably, but not for long. Football in Spain is rooted in local, regional and national pride, passion and commitment. So much so that many debtors let the clubs off and wiped the slate clean.

In Brazil, some of the greatest clubs in the world have had their tax debts sponged out by the government. It has allowed the clubs a breather at least. They have also been given a shot in the arm by the 2010 South African World Cup. To prepare for the World Cup, some top Brazilian players have returned home on loan from clubs abroad. The great "Robinho" Robson de Souza delighted Santos fans when he joined the club on loan from Manchester City.

In Brazil such players can practise their own national style of the game — and hopefully catch the eye of their Football Association's selectors! For Brazil's clubs it means bigger gates as fans flock to see their homecoming heroes. It means much-needed money from merchandising. But clubs across the globe are feeling the pinch. How can football jump off this money merry-go-round?

FAIR PLAY TO THEM

UEFA have had enough. They have launched a Financial Fairplay Initiative. Clubs that get into debt by overborrowing to buy the best players are now in serious trouble. They will no longer be allowed to compete in UEFA's great competitions such as the Champions' League.

Owners are speaking out, too. David Gold, one of West Ham's owners since 2009, declared that overborrowing to pay for the best players is simply cheating. Let's not forget that the best players win cups and help clubs to the top of the league. This in turn brings more money to a club to buy even better players. Gold wants fairer play.

But there are examples of fair play in football. Perhaps the cup for fairest play of all goes to those clubs that in spite of their debt help other clubs that are less well off.

Beckham's goodwill

And what about David Beckham, one of the wealthiest footballers of all time? He has set up football academies in the more deprived districts of Los Angeles and England's East End of London, where he was born. Since 2005 Beckham has also worked as a UNESCO goodwill ambassador on projects such as Malaria No More.

Barcelona spends a lot of cash in Rwanda, once a war-torn country. Here, the club has helped 19 000 young people into sport and out of trouble. It works with the UNHCR to provide access to education, housing and health. As Barcelona's President, Joan Laporta said, "Barcelona is more than just a club."

NAMES OF PASSION

Money talks. New football grounds and stadiums across the world are being renamed by the sponsors who financed them. So now these venues could be named after anything from a bank to a brand of washing machine.

Stadiums used to be named in a ceremonious way. Some after famous footballers, others after national heroes or local historical sites that supporters are proud of. And through love and passion, fans have also fondly given them nicknames, like:

- Argentina's Boca Juniors play in Buenos Aires in "The Chocolate Box";
- Also in Buenos Aires, the Sarsfield Stadium is known as "The Fort";
- In Scotland, Glasgow's Celtic Park is "Paradise";
- Greece's Karaiskakis Stadium in Piraeus is called "The Frying Pan";
- In Mexico's Hidalgo State, the Estadio Hidalgo must be a bit blowy, fans name it "The Hurricane";

• In Veracruz, Estadio Luis de la Fuente is called "The Pirate";

• In the Netherlands, Feijenoord in Rotterdam play in an affectionately named "The Tub"; and

• Turkey's Ali Sami Yen stadium in Istanbul is "The Hell". So many are.

NEW NAME, A BIT OF A PROBLEM

FIFA has a list of official sponsors. But not all sponsors of stadiums are associated with FIFA, and so are "unofficial sponsors". If a stadium is named by an unofficial sponsor, then a temporary name has to be used during a FIFA competition. So at the 2006 World Cup in Germany, the Allianz Arena in Munich (Munchen) was renamed FIFA World Cup Stadium, Munich. And for UEFA European competitions, it is known as the Munchen Arena. This unique stadium, which looks like a massive iced ring doughnut, will hold the Allianz name for 30 years, from 2005. After that time the name could be changed yet again by a new sponsor. There should be no problem attracting investment to this great footballing city — a magnet for sponsors!

THE OPENING CEREMONY OF THE ALLIANZ ARENA IN MUNICH, GERMANY, ON 31 MAY 2005.
THE STADIUM HAS A TOTAL SEATING CAPACITY OF 59416.

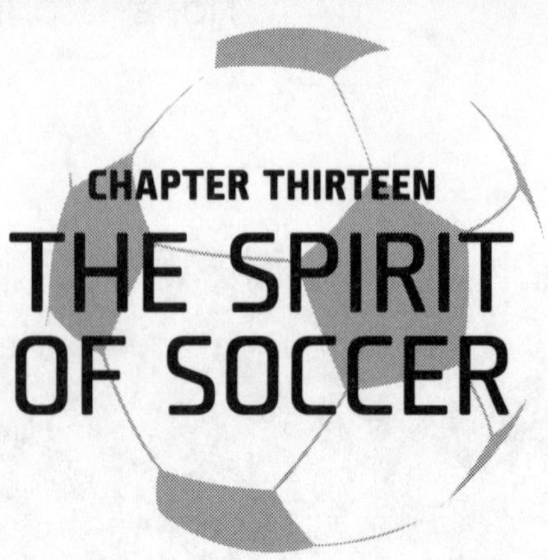

CHAPTER THIRTEEN

THE SPIRIT OF SOCCER

THE SPIRIT OF SOCCER lies in its drive to conquer all obstacles, in the stellar talents of its players, and in the tenacity of its supporters. But is this soccer spirit always good and well-intentioned? Well, sometimes yes, and at other times definitely not.

SOCCER AND SALSA

In Brazil's capital, Rio de Janeiro, the *carioca* are waving in unison; singing in deafening disharmony. They're some of the wildest, most exhilarating supporters in the world. And "real" *carioca* are from just three clubs — Flamengo, Botafogo or Fluminense. All are passionate to the point of obsession — and it is said they are more loyal to their club than to their own spouse, more loving than to their own mother. Why? Because each team represents not only a part of the city, but also its class, culture and history.

Traditionally, Botafogo is the team of the middle classes; Flamengo's fans are poorer, while Fluminense *carioca* are from the rich upper classes. But this is football — and football never stands still. You will now find supporters crossing the social and cultural divide to follow the team of their dreams. And this mixing is happening gradually in supporters' clubs all over the world.

Brazil's *carioca* show just how important football is as a raw emotional expression of politics, religion and social class. Like Uruguay and Argentina, Brazilian football rivalry is based on "derbys" — matches between clubs within one city rather than between different cities, something well-known in England's Manchester and in Scotland's Glasgow, where modern football began. What could be more nerve-racking and magnetic than a Glasgow derby? The clash between blue-and-white Rangers and green-and-white Celtic — rooted in the divisions between Protestant Glasgow and Catholic Glasgow. But is this manic rivalry a good thing? Doesn't it just fuel the worst aspects of soccer?

Soccer support can show the very best spirit of football — the cheering and the carolling, but it also shows its very worst — with ugly verbal abuse, brawling, missile-hurling and depressingly, the occasional death. Without supporters, though, how could football possibly conquer the world? Football clubs have united communities and divided societies, and they continue to generate debate in papers and parliaments across the globe.

Enmeshed in the mix of many soccer debates is that most poisonous of spirits — racism. Over the decades, racism has seeped into every corner of the footballing world — on the field, in the dressing room and on the terraces. But it doesn't have to be this way. Let's look back to modern football's beginnings, to see how the positive spirit of the game can be realised, and how one talented footballer conquered his world.

ANDREW WATSON – A SCOTTISH SOCCER LEGEND

Andrew Watson was born on a sugar plantation in Demerara, British Guiana, in 1857 — far from the emerging world of football. He was the son of Peter Miller, a wealthy plantation owner — and Rose Watson, a local young African-American woman. At fourteen, young Andrew sailed across the Atlantic to the posh King's College, London. Here he showed huge promise in a wide range of sports. But Watson was smart as well as sporty. At nineteen he got a place at Glasgow University to study

Shaming the game

There has never been an official enquiry into Belgium's Heysel Stadium tragedy. It took place at the European Cup final on 29th May 1985 between Liverpool and Juventus, and involved violent scenes involving both sets of football supporters. Thirty-nine people died – thirty-two Italians, four Belgians and an Irishman.

philosophy, mathematics and engineering (and to play an awful lot of football!).

Andrew Watson was one of the first footballers to combine playing with soccer administration. And because he always an amateur, Watson played for the famous Corinthians in 1884 — the first foreign-born footballer to be invited. He was even capped three times for Scotland, captaining the side that defeated England 6–1 in 1884.

Eventually, Andrew Watson took his wife and children to that great sporting city of Sydney, Australia. There, he lies buried — but not forgotten. An entry in the 1880–81 Scottish FA *Annual* says of Watson: "One of the very best backs we have … has great speed and tackles splendidly; powerful and sure kick; well worthy of a place in any representative team."

Watson was never hailed as the first black soccer star in Britain — because the colour of his skin wasn't an issue. The only colour associated with this distinguished player was his brown boots — most players wore black in those days. So what's happened since? African players have been given a very rough ride on many teams and in front of many crowds across the globe. So, too, have players who've tried to fight political injustice through their sport.

POLITICS ON THE PITCH?

Does the spirit of soccer mix with politics? Many believe it doesn't. But what if you're trying to play under a cruel regime? What if there are protests all around you against the injustices of the world? What should footballers do then? Some have stuck their necks out big-time to show that soccer can speak for those who have no voice.

Socrates Brasileiro Sampaio de Souza Vieira de Oliveira (1954–), or more simply, just "Socrates", was for many years the midfield star of Brazil and Sao Paolo's giants — the Corinthians. But he is also a qualified doctor, a philosopher and a freedom fighter. Brazil was under a dictatorship through much of Socrates' time in first-class football. And he never lost an opportunity to spell out his opposition to it — often literally with slogans on his shirts. He believed passionately that he could change the world and play soccer at the same time.

The Sunshine Cup

What a triumph! World Cup 2010 was handed to football-mad South Africa. Here the spirit of soccer shone through decades of apartheid — a system that only recognised the rights of white people. Black and coloured South Africans had to practise and play on earth pitches with few facilities and no money. "I feel like I'm fifteen again," cried Nelson Mandela, in his 80s, when he heard that South Africa would host the Cup.

"I'm struggling for freedom, for respect for human beings, for ample and unrestricted discussions … and all of this as a soccer player."

SOCCER NATIONS UNDER THE SPOTLIGHT

Political issues and scandals seem to follow football everywhere, suffocating the soccer spirit. But with such intrusive, hyped media interest, how many rumours are true? Time and time again FIFA members and officials have been accused of corruption. Of manipulating the selection of particular nations to host the lucrative World Cup competitions. And wicked whispers have followed many a "strange" World Cup match result. Every tournament has faced its share of flak.

The 1954 tournament was held in Switzerland — chocolate-box pretty, politically neutral Switzerland. No problems there, then? The tournament ran well, and the final thrilled the crowd with five goals — West Germany beat boiling-hot favourites Hungary 3–2. But afterwards many of the winning West German players disappeared for a while with unknown ailments. Rumours were

---

Punished for politics

The English football association punished Liverpool and England's Robbie Fowler in 1997 for mixing soccer with politics. He wore a slogan on his undershirt supporting unemployed dockworkers. The FA gave him a suspension and a fine.

---

rife. Had they taken drugs? Or were they just physical wrecks? I mean, you'd feel a bit tired after winning a World Cup, wouldn't you?

Their Hungarian opponents had other problems. Communist USSR was getting tough on its Central European states — the USSR's buffer zone with the capitalist West. Hungary wanted to break free from hard-line communism — to let the economy and the people breathe a little; to be more like their Western neighbours. But the USSR was having none of it. In October 1956, USSR's tanks rolled into Hungary's capital, Budapest, in a vicious clampdown on political activists. Many of Hungary's artists, scholars and soccer stars fled. Hungary's communist sports system had created its own superstars and a unique training system through lavish investment. Western clubs would now reap the benefits: the great Puskas joined Real Madrid, and Czibor went to Barcelona.

Soccer sorrow

Tragedy has struck the game many times. In 1949, Italy's tremendous Torino club team were all killed in an air crash on their way home from a friendly. Ten Torino players had played for Italy, twice winners of the World Cup. Then in 1958, Manchester United's "Busby Babes" were involved in a crash that killed twenty-three people – and eight Man U players. From the survivors, Bobby Charlton went on to help England win the 1966 World Cup.

But what about the anguish of matches won and lost among claims of foul play and "blind" referees? What about Geoff Hurst's second goal against West Germany in the epic 1966 World Cup final? Did the ball go over the goal line after hitting the crossbar, or didn't it? And England's agony in the 1986 World Cup quarter finals? Was Maradona's first goal scored with the help of his arm, or as Maradona himself put it, "the hand of God"?

The pressure of politics both on and in the game rests with the various football associations and FIFA. But the pressure of split-second decisions on the pitch itself lands squarely on the shoulders of those tireless troopers: the refs. Often vainly, they try to keep the true spirit of sportsmanship alive.

TAMING THE GAME

"The referee was booking everyone. I thought he was filling in his lottery card."

Ian Wright: player for Arsenal and England

"I believe in the traditional role of accepting decisions as part of the discipline of sportsmanship and fair play."

Pierluigi Collina: international referee

We've come a long way from the early-19th century free-for-all football brawls. And we've moved on from mid-19th century polite self-regulation: "It's your free kick, Henry", "No, you take it Charles — I'm sure it's yours." Today, there's a referee and two assistant referees — replacing umpires and linesmen. There are even experiments taking place in Italy with two referees on the pitch. Will this work? Football officials are unsure — they're a cautious bunch. There are other things to worry about too, like whether or not refs should go professional, or if there should be a cricket-style "third umpire". And there are so many issues on the pitch itself — like shirt-tugging, elbowing, diving … the tacky tricks are endless.

But if there's one person who can sort out these sins, it's Pierluigi Collina. Collina is one of the most famous faces on the pitch, but not as a player. Italian Collina, born in 1960, started training as a referee when he was only seventeen. He refereed his first Serie A match in 1991; his first Olympic match in 1996; and his first World Cup in 1998. Collina speaks Italian, English, Spanish and French. So footballers can't really pretend they don't understand what he's saying! But Collina is just as powerful when he says nothing at all. His charisma comes from his confidence and a deep understanding of football and its players.

PIERLUIGI COLLINA, SUPER-REF

Even Collina, though, finds battling under the media's spotlight a struggle. It's all so easy from the journalist's point of view — if you're up in the TV producer's box with every on-screen view of the pitch at your disposal. Super-ref Collina admits he "can't fight television", reminding everyone that, "each game at Euro 2000 was covered by eighteen different cameras from eighteen different positions." Now that's pressure! Modern media certainly stirs up the mix when we're arguing whether the ref got it right.

Collina reached FIFA's retirement age of 45 in 2005. But for the great Collina, the rules were adjusted slightly. He refereed his final international, between Portugal and Slovakia, at Lisbon's Stadium of Light in 2006. Since then he has taken to the pitch for the occasional charity match but his advice will most likely be sought for many years to come. One more thing about Collina. As a young man he wisely took a university degree in Economics and now has a successful career as a financial advisor. So at 45 years of age he was not left high and dry. A good example of why it is wise to never neglect your studies!

"Swedes 2, Turnips 1"
Britain's *Sun* newspaper cruelly spelled gloom for Graham Taylor when his England team played Sweden in a 1992 European Cup qualifier. The English played abysmally – yes, that's them – the "Turnips". And the great Gary Lineker, one-time winner of the Golden Boot, crept dismally off the pitch in this, his last international. Taylor had substituted this brilliant striker in the second half, even though a goal was vital.

SPREADING SOCCER

The media has played its part in helping football to conquer the world, despite creating difficulties for the refs. From its infancy in the 1860s, organised soccer was reported in the sporting press — and soon it outpaced the interest in horseracing. Photography was well-developed by then. So football arrived just as media and printed images were beginning to create celebrities. The successes and scandals of the modern game were with us almost from day one … and then came soccer on the screen.

It's a dead ball
Television transmits some terrifying moments. And some terrifyingly funny moments. Like when a South American football fan ran onto the pitch brandishing a gun – and shot … the ball!

Filmed football was first seen as highlights on Britain's Pathé News and screened in cinemas. But on 9 April 1938, an international between England and Scotland was shown on that rare object, the television. By 1958, televisions were taking over sitting rooms, and many people watched the first screening of the World Cup. Since then, soccer has been beamed across the globe and bounced off satellite dishes. In 1970, the World Cup competition dazzled us in glorious telly technicolour.

The media both past and present has been hugely responsible for creating soccer superstars. But journalists and the paparazzo have made their names (and money) by building players up and then cruelly pulling them down.

DAVID BECKHAM IN ACTION FOR REAL MADRID 2003

Football on film

Films such as Britain's *Bend it like Beckham* have brought football to new audiences in many parts of the world – conquering even the US, where American football (grid-iron) reigns supreme. *Bend it like Beckham* even kick-started a whole new football film-fest, including the blockbuster, *Goal!*

CHAPTER FOURTEEN FOOTBALL FOREVER!

"To the great majority of these [football players and supporters], football is one of the prime interests of life, sometimes an all-consuming interest, without which life would scarcely be worth living."

Morris Marples (1954): sports' scholar, historian and writer

HOW DO WE KEEP football alive for its devoted fans and for the generations to come? What's left for the game? Where will it go next? The challenge now seems to be to find ways of making football even more accessible. To find versions of the game that can be played in tighter spaces and remoter places — by people with different abilities and personal challenges, people of different ages and stages in life. When the game is opened up to all sections of society, and is played in peace and with good humour, then surely it will have conquered the world. And wasn't that the dream of all those football pioneers so long ago?

HOW FAR HAVE WE COME?

On the sun-kissed sands of Rio, a melee of men is booting a ball toward a distant goal. Scrabbling, scrambling, tangling and tackling they chase the ball as it thuds and skids along the grit.

"Mine!"

"No, it's MINE!"

"Too late! GOOOOAL!'

Hang on a minute! Isn't this how we began? Only wasn't it 4000 years ago on a beach in Greece? Has anything really changed since then? You could say that everything has changed, because since ancient Greek times, football has conquered most of the globe. But it's also true that nothing has changed, because a ball is still being belted along a beach. Perhaps it is just a new era, but there is still another twist to this football fable.

The men kicking a ball along a beach are taking part in the very first FIFA Beach Soccer World Cup. Held in Rio in 2005, this new championship competition takes place

---

Brazil's skills

Brazil's Football Institute (BFUT) is at the forefront of football excellence. It spearheads training – from Socatots' sessions for the Under-5s, to Player Profiles for the professionals. These profiles analyse a player's abilities in four main areas: psychomotor development (that just means "physical"!), psychological aspects, technical analysis and tactical. This is very serious stuff.

---

on a challenging surface with truly talented players. Football is obviously alive and well, conquering new surfaces, new techniques, a whole new pantheon of players and a huge wave of young supporters.

Beach soccer is a thrilling five-a-side, one-touch game played on compacted sand. Its footballers are barefoot and fast-kicking. Its famous followers, players and coaches include one-time France and Manchester United hero, Eric Cantona. And it was France, trained by Cantona, who proudly held the Beach Soccer World Cup trophy aloft on 16 May 2005. They'd defeated Portugal in an epic match. The final score line was 3–3, but France just snatched it on heart-thumping penalties.

In 2009 Brazil won its fourth tournament in a row — this time in Dubai. They trounced newcomers Switzerland 10-5 in the final. But the Swiss player Dejan Stankovic took the Golden Shoe award for the best player of the tournament — for his heading, scoring and speed.

This game-in-the-sand now marches alongside another dynamic five-a-side game, futsal. More commonly known as Futebol de Salao, or "hall football", it was devised in 1930 by a Uruguayan PE instructor, Juan Carlos Ceriani. As a teacher, he was conscious that many young people had to play football in small spaces and on hard surfaces. So he developed a game that would suit these conditions and encourage young people to play with discipline.

As with football codes and practices through the ages, the game spread. It was adopted and adapted with great flare by young people on the streets of the city of Sao Paulo in Brazil.

FIFA noticed futsal's popularity and realised that as the game could be played indoors, it would make football accessible to more people. It was fast, too, which encourages excellent, dramatic footwork and ball skills — and lightning reactions. Great players of today — Kaka, Fabregas, Ronaldo and Robinho — have all cut their teeth on futsal. In 1989 FIFA organised its first Futsal World Cup in the Netherlands. Brazil won. They raised the cup in the 2008 competition held in Rio de Janeiro, too. But Brazil have not had things all their own way. Spain have managed to take the trophy a couple of times in between!

OH YES! FOOTBALL IS CONQUERING THE WORLD

There are over 250 million registered soccer players worldwide. Thirty billion people follow football on the small screen, and FIFA now recognises 207 national teams — that's more countries than belong to the United Nations! These teams are affiliated to one of six regional confederations that cover the organisation and development of football across the globe:

- AFC Asian Football Confederation — in Asia;

- CAF Confederation Africaine de Football — in Africa;
- CONMEBOL Confederacion Sudamericana de Futbol — in South America;
- OFC Oceania Football Confederation — in Australia and Oceania; and
- UEFA Union of European Football Federations — in Europe.

Some countries span or border more than one region. Turkey and Russia, for example, could be in Asia or Europe. So they're allowed to belong to the organisation of their choice. Both belong to UEFA. Many new nations are developing their own football identities, such as Kazakhstan, which has also made the move from AFC to UEFA.

THE SLEEPING DRAGON

A torrent of talent is about to hit the footballing world. And it's coming from China — with its 1.1 billion potential players and supporters. Its fanatical fan base already buys into the world's most famous footballers — from Ronaldo and Rooney to Kaka amd Messi. But in spite of their love of international stars, China's soccer supporters are crying for some of their own.

As we've seen before, national politics often steers the direction of football. In China, politics has also been responsible for soccer's stop-start history. The Communist Revolution in 1949 shut the door on full international competition, as China closed in on itself. Yet football didn't fade away. In fact, from 1953, China's players were nurtured in their own excellent Sports' Institutes. This massive, unwieldy nation was beginning to centralise its game through its elite training centres.

But China's political clashes with other nations continued to leave her out in the cold. For many years the rest of the footballing world almost lost sight of her. Encouraged patiently by FIFA, China finally joined the Asian Football Conference in 1976 and became a full member of FIFA in 1980.

The Chinese Football Association saw that a strong national team needs a vibrant club league system to sustain it. So in 1994 its Professional Soccer League kicked off. The talent and competitiveness pushed teams to another level. To cope with it, the China Football Association Super League was formed in

---

Back to basics

Cameroon's "Indomitable Lions" have roared like no other African side. They are the only African nation to take part in four World Cups, and to reach the quarter finals. They even won the 2000 Sydney Olympic gold medal, but their talented stars then lost to West Africa's Mali 1–0 in a 2006 World Cup qualifer. So now it's back to basics for Cameroon. Meanwhile, Mali and other lesser-known African soccer nations will freshen the international scene.

SOCCEROO MARK SCHWARZER, AUSTRALIA V URUGUAY, 2005

2004. And its members will see a lot of international club competition in the future — especially within the Asian Football Confederation.

China's football organisers now welcome foreign players and managers with open arms. They're already improving standards of play and helping to create homegrown soccer legends of the future. But like many other emerging soccer nations, China knows that developing superstars is risky. For they will doubtless be tempted by the "greener pastures" of top clubs in other parts of the world.

Recently, China's long-term ambitions took

a nose-dive when she failed to qualify for both the 2006 and 2010 World Cups. Stung by the disappointment, this fast-growing footballing nation is determined to compete much more successfully and has qualified for the 2011 AFC tournament. China's football is creative and when the team becomes more comfortable and confident in its attack it will shoot forward from its capable defence and start really scoring. Watch out, though! Although China is poised to ride the crest of the world soccer wave, the newest AFC member will be trying its best to make life hard for her.

MOVING ON UP

Football fans might idolise the brilliance of the Brazilians and the magic of the Italians, but other nations are quietly riding the football funicular. After thirty-two years in World Cup wilderness, Australia's national team took to the big stage. Yes, in 2006 the Socceroos went on their way to Germany for only their second World Cup appearance in the Cup's history.

To qualify, the Socceroos needed to be the highest ranked team from the OFC. But their trials weren't over. They then had to play the fifth-ranked team from the South American grouping. For the second time in a row, in World Cup qualifying rounds, the Socceroos had to play the much more experienced Uruguayans. But this time they dug in and defeated the South Americans after a heart-thumping penalty shoot out. At the 2006 World Cup Australia reached the round of sixteen — a great result. They made it through qualifying to a tough group in the 2010 World Cup, too. It is quite an ask to play for a result against Serbia, Ghana and Germany but the Socceroos are always determined to show their worth.

Part of the team's new success is due to their move from the OFC to the AFC in 2006. This gave them keener competition and a much smoother route to the World Cup. They're leaping ahead, and moves are being made by Football Federation Australia to encourage home-grown stars to stay in their country, and to play in the newly established A-League. Local stars mean better clubs, and a truly competitive national team. Australia's star is set to rise.

NEVER GIVE UP!

Which country started the world's first indoor soccer league in 1923 and shocked the World Cup in 1950 by beating England 1–0? And which club has never really made it into the top echelons of men's football? Yes, it's the US, where teams such as New York Cosmos signed stars like Pelé (in 1974). Yet nothing yielded results, until … Bruce Arena took charge of the international team in 1998. It then reached the round of sixteen in the 2002

World Cup and qualified for Germany 2006. There was no repeat of the 2002 success, though, as the US were beaten 2-1 by Ghana at the Group stage. Bruce Arena's assistant, Bob Bradley, took over as manager, and helped his team to a comfortable ride into the World Cup 2010. It is time for them to break through. They're definitely on the way up.

And this is surely one of the greatest fascinations of modern football. That teams and players rise and fall. They ebb and flow. They belong to a world pulsating with triumphs and tragedies, stars and has-beens, sinners and saints. Just when you think that nothing new will happen, a team surges from nowhere, storming up a league — its unknown supporters bringing new team colours, cheeky chants and belting ballads to those cathedrals of dreams.

Post script

Utter humiliation! As this book goes to press, my beloved Stockport County are indeed in the stocks. For they're dangling at the bottom of England's Coca Cola Championship League One — and they only moved up there this season. Far too much gung-ho celebration at the time in my mind. Relegation looms. But hope lies around the corner: There's ALWAYS NEXT SEASON! They're the "Hatters" for goodness sake! They will never lie down and die.

ACKNOWLEDGEMENTS

To my father, who encouraged us kids to watch soccer on our black and white TV screen. The lack of colour focussed our eyes on the skills, but gave no clue as to which team was which. To my son, Michael King, whose knowledge and wit led me to explore aspects of the game totally outside my thoughtspan. And whose undying passion for Chelsea FC and Italy in the 1990s made me cast aside memories of the skill-starved scrums of rather too many 1970s matches, and turn once more to the great game. Finally, to the soccer enthusiasts who tried to make me write about their team alone. You drove me mad, but reminded me constantly just how powerful and important the game is to so many, from all walks of life.

GLOSSARY

ADVANTAGE RULE

The referee lets play carry on after a foul without stopping to give a free kick if this will give an advantage to the side fouled.

ATTACKING MIDFIELDER

The midfield player who hovers just behind the attacking forwards. He sets up a lot of the forward play and sometimes even scores a goal!

BANANA KICK

You guessed — a ball that swerves a lot. Achieved by kicking in a certain way with the inside of the foot it sometimes ends in a spectacular goal.

BICYCLE KICK

Very impressive! A player with his back to the net kicks the ball in mid air and backwards over his own head. It has resulted in a goal, too.

BREAKAWAY

An attacker zooms off ahead with the ball, with no-one between him and the goalkeeper. True gladiator stuff.

CAUTION

This is when a player fouls badly enough to get a Yellow Card.

CENTRE SPOT

A spot in the centre of the pitch on which the first kick of the match starts. Also where the match restarts after a goal is scored. The spot is surrounded by a wide circle.

CHIP PASS

A short, sharp kick of the ball over a defender's head towards a team mate.

CHIP SHOT

A short, sharp kick of the ball aimed just over the goalkeeper or other defender's head and hopefully into the back of the net.

CUT OFF

A defender blocks an attacker with a ball so well that the attacker has to take the ball wide.

DEFENSIVE MIDFIELDER

A player at the front of his team's defence. He often marks the other side's attacking genius. Often a hard, thankless task.

DEFLECTION

When the ball is kicked and bounces off a player's body.

DIRECT FREE KICK

A kick given to a team after a serious foul by the opposition. No opposing team members are allowed within ten yards of the free kick. A goal can be scored from this.

DIVING HEADER

A ball headed by a player diving close to the ground.

FEINT, FEIGN, FAKE!

A false movement by a player with the ball to wrong-foot the opposition.

FORMATION

How a team arranges its players — goalkeeper excluded. So a 4-4-2 formation is 4 defenders, 4 midfielders and 2 forwards. These days many teams have a more complicated formation, such as 4-1-2-1-2. This 'diamond' shape formation means that midfielders have to be really flexible.

FRONT HEADER

Striking the ball with the forehead.

FRONT TACKLE

When a player faces his opponent and tries to take the ball.

FULL BACK

A defender who plays close to the goalkeeper.

GOAL KICK

When the game is restarted with a kick up the pitch by the goalkeeper. It occurs after the opposing team has put the ball across the goal line — but not in the goal itself!

HACKING

Kicking a player's legs or feet. Just "No", really.

HALFBACK

A defender who works behind the attackers and in front of the fullbacks.

HAND BALL

A foul by a player — not the goalkeeper — who touches the ball with his hand or arm.

INDIRECT FREE KICK

Like a direct free kick but awarded for a less serious foul. The other players still have to stand 10 yards from the player taking the free kick. But a goal can only be scored if it touches another player first.

JUGGLING

Keeping the ball in the air using the legs, feet, chest, head — and even the back! But not, of course, the hand or arm.

LINKMEN

Usually midfielders, who develop play between the defenders and the attackers.

MAN-TO-MAN OR ONE-ON-ONE

A defender who is given just one forward player from the opposing team to mark closely throughout the match.

OBSTRUCTION

When a player blocks his opponent's body without trying to play the ball.

OFFSIDE

A foul committed by a player who receives a passed ball with less than two opposing players between him and the goalkeeper.

OPEN

An attacking player with no player from the opposing team marking him.

OUT OF PLAY

When the ball is outside the boundaries of the pitch or the referee has stopped play.

OVERLAP

When a winger — an attacking player close to the side lines — rushes to the centre of the field allowing a team mate to zip up the sideline with the ball. The winger often draws the other team's defenders with him.

PENALTY AREA

A large rectangle marked around the goal. The goalkeeper is only allowed to handle the ball within this area. Outside the area he has to kick like anyone else.

PENALTY KICK

A kick awarded to the attacking team for a serious violation of rules by the defending team within the penalty area. Or, when a player commits any type of foul and already has one yellow card given for a foul. The kick allows a player to shoot at goal 12 yards (11 metres) from a spot away from the goal with only the goalkeeper in front of him.

POSSESSION

The player and his team with the ball at any one time. "Keeping possession" is hugely important as it allows a team to build up towards a goal.

PROFESSIONAL FOUL

A foul committed on purpose to stop an almost certain goal but without giving away a penalty. Cunning but not clever.

PUSH PASS

A pass made by pushing the ball with the inside of the foot rather than kicking it. It can be very accurate and subtle, too.

RED CARD

A Red Card waved at a player by the referee for a really serious foul or receiving a second Yellow Card.

SCREENING OR SHIELDING

When a player with possession of the ball shields it from an opposing player with neat movement of the body.

SET PLAY

Moves planned before the game to build up ball possession or score a goal. Often made for certain situations like a direct or indirect free kick or a throw-in.

SIDELINE OR TOUCHLINE

The lines marking the length of the pitch.

SIDE TACKLE

A player tackling an opponent who has the ball by running alongside him and reaching the ball with his foot to tap it away.

SLIDING TACKLE

A player tackling an opponent who has the ball by skidding towards the ball feet first — hoping to make contact with the ball and not the player. It often ends in a foul!

SQUARE PASS

A sideways pass made to a team mate positioned level with him.

SWEEPER

A single defender who plays just in front of the goalkeeper, moving across the width of the field to protect the goal.

THROUGH PASS

A pass sent well ahead of the player's team mates to bypass defenders. The hope is that an attacker will run on to the ball and move straight toward goal.

THROW-IN

When a game is restarted with the ball thrown from the sideline after the ball has been put out of play by the opposing team.

VOLLEY

A ball kicked while it is in the air.

WALL

A line of defenders trying to stop the ball from the opposing team's free kick.

WINGERS

Forwards who play up and down the sidelines.

YELLOW CARD

A Yellow Card held up by the referee after a foul committed outside the penalty area. Or when a player is not behaving nicely! Two "yellow" players make a Red Card — which is pretty final!

REFERENCES

BOOKS

Davies, Hunter, *Boots, Balls and Haircuts*, Cassell Illustrated, 2003.

A great read on all aspects of footballing history — I especially like the chapter on football merchandise, which could fill a book all by itself.

Goldblatt, David, *The Ball is Round: A Global History of Soccer*, Penguin, 2008.

You'll need your kitbag to carry this tome, which is nearly 1 000 pages-worth of world soccer history. A great work, it clearly matches each change in the game to its place in history and society, And you can dip in and out of it, too.

Harris, Harry, *Vialli — Diary of His Season*, Orion, 2000.

Biographies give a really detailed insight into individual clubs as well as individual players or managers. This one is a bit different from some. The diary format really pulls you into the ins and outs of a fine footballing hero and a great club, Chelsea FC.

Marples, Morris, *A History of Football*, Secker and Warburg, 1955.

My favourite source, as Marples truly realises the global impact of soccer, and how each nation and culture carves its own stamp and style on the game. He predicts, rightly, the rise of African nations, from his observations in the 1950s of their passion and flair.

Strutt, Joseph, *Sports and Pastimes of the People of England* first published in 1801, revised in 1868 and 1903, published by William Tutt.

This is a fascinating peek into England's sporting life and all kinds of merriment. It actually shows how soccer was holding on by a thread in the first part of the 19th century, just waiting to morph from a kickabout into a king of sports.

WEBSITES

Every great club has its own official website where you can find out all you need to know about your favourite team, its players and its aims.

But for me, the best website is:

www.fifa.com

This is the beating heart of world football. I learn so much about the game, from the greatest stadiums to the remotest village pitches in the world. From the game's great triumphs to FIFA's agonies over the challenges that soccer continues to throw up.

INDEX

ALSO BY CATHERINE CHAMBERS

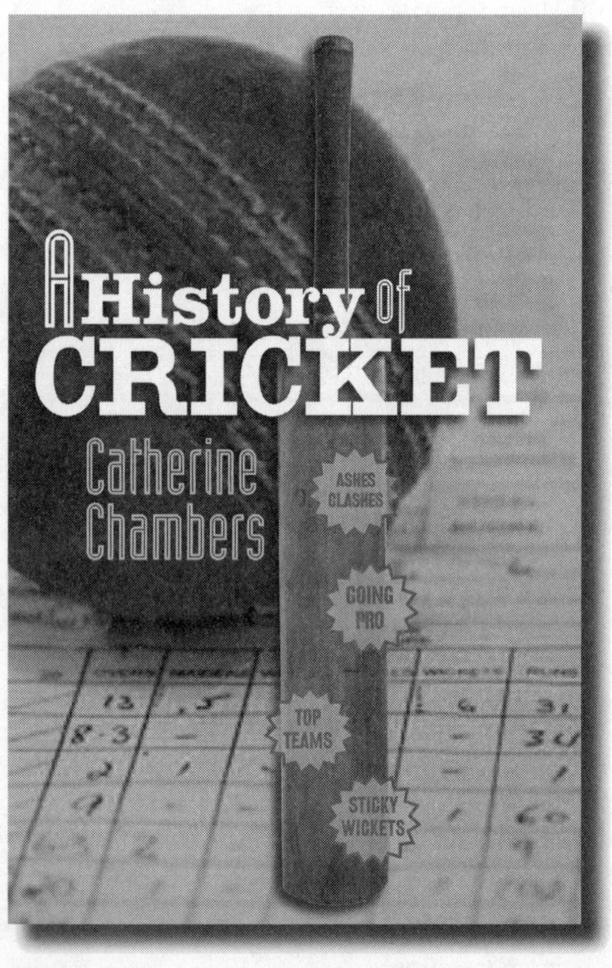

A HISTORY OF CRICKET

For millions of fans worldwide, cricket is the world.

But how did this game that has too many rules and can take days to play take hold in every corner of the globe?

This is the history of the quirkiest sport on the planet.

Any other sport is just not cricket!

For backyard cricketers, aspiring national heroes — and everyone in between.

A History of Cricket is an Eve Pownall Notable Book of 2010 — The Children's Book Council of Australia.

REVIEW

"This book is a very comprehensive account of this most noble game. It will be enjoyed by all, from the backyard cricketers to those aspiring to don the baggy green."

— *Good Reading*, February 2010

ABOUT THE AUTHOR

Catherine Chambers was born in Adelaide and was shaken but not stirred by an earthquake that hit the city four hours later. She has lived in Nigeria, Portugal and England where similar disturbances have occurred. Catherine took a degree in African History and Swahili and then entered the world of publishing. She enjoys writing about history, cultures and religions — and reckons that sport can satisfy all three. She loves traveling, but never as much as the times when she and her family chugged across Europe in their old VW bus.